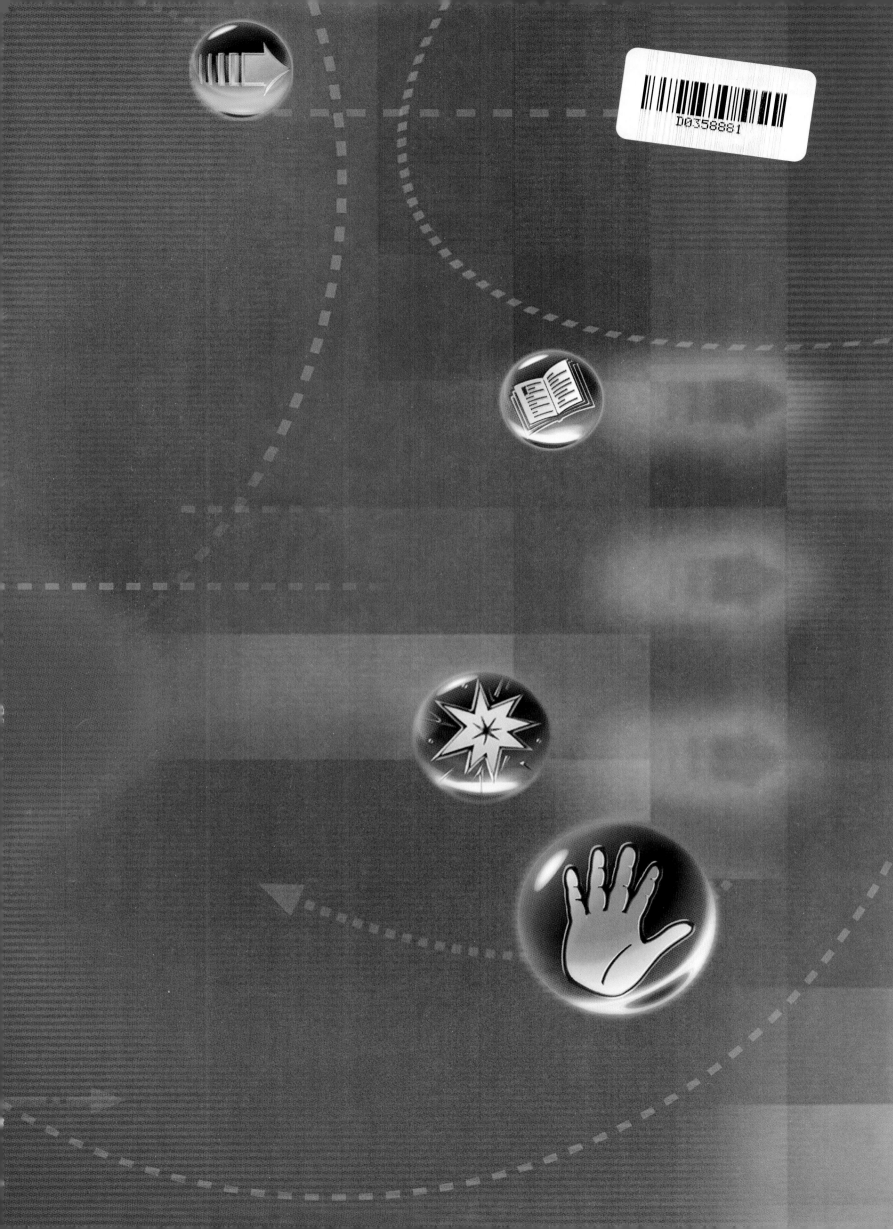

# THE READER'S DIGEST
## Children's Book of

# Sharks
## and Other Sea Creatures

# 𝒯HE READER'S DIGEST
## Children's Book of
# Sharks
## and Other Sea Creatures

A Reader's Digest® Children's Book,
published 2000 by Reader's Digest Children's Publishing Ltd,
King's Court, Parsonage Lane, Bath BA1 1ER,
a subsidiary of The Reader's Digest Association, Inc.

Conceived and produced by Weldon Owen Pty Limited
59 Victoria Street, McMahons Point, NSW, 2060, Australia
A member of the Weldon Owen Group of Companies
Sydney • San Francisco

© 2000 Weldon Owen Inc.

READER'S DIGEST CHILDREN'S BOOKS
President: Vivian Antonangeli
Group Publisher: Rosanna Hansen
Managing Editor: Cathy Jones
Editors: Louise Pritchard and Annabel Blackledge
Assistant Editor: Sarah Williams

WELDON OWEN PTY LTD
Chief Executive Officer: John Owen
President: Terry Newell
Publisher: Sheena Coupe
Associate Publisher: Lynn Humphries
Art Director: Sue Burk
Consultant, Design Concept and Cover Design: John Bull
Design Concept: Clare Forte, Robyn Latimer
Editorial Assistants: Sarah Anderson, Tracey Jackson
Production Manager: Helen Creeke
Production Assistant: Kylie Lawson
Vice President International Sales: Stuart Laurence

Author: Leighton Taylor
Consultant: Sylvia James
Project Editors: Emma Marks, Janine Flew
Designers: James Marks, Cliff Watt
Picture Research: Amanda Weir, Annette Crueger

Illustrators: Martin Camm, Marjorie Crosby-Fairall, Marc Dando/Wildlife Art Ltd., Ray Grinaway,
Gino Hasler, Ian Jackson/Wildlife Art Ltd., Roger Swainston, Chris Turnbull/Wildlife Art Ltd.

British Library Cataloguing in Publication Data.
A catalogue record for this book is available
from the British Library.

Colour Reproduction by Colourscan Co Pte Ltd
Printed by Tien Wah Press Pte Ltd
Printed in Singapore

A WELDON OWEN PRODUCTION

# THE READER'S DIGEST
## Children's Book of

# Sharks
## and Other Sea Creatures

*A Reader's Digest Children's Book*

# Contents

## Introducing...Sharks 6

## Sharkworks 26

## A Shark's World 46

# Pick Your Path!

READY FOR A swim with *Sharks and Other Sea Creatures*? Plunge into the pages of this book for a look at some of nature's most efficient underwater predators. Cruise straight through with the gentle giants of the shark world, then come face to face with the scariest shark of them all – the great white. Or, if you want to find out more about a subject, use the 'Pathfinder'.

You'll find plenty of other discovery paths to choose from in the special features sections. Read about real-life shark experts in 'Inside Story', or get creative with 'Hands On' activities. Delve into words with 'Word Builders', or amaze your friends with fascinating facts from 'That's Amazing!' You can choose a new path with every reading - THE READER'S DIGEST CHILDREN'S BOOK OF SHARKS AND OTHER SEA CREATURES will take you where *you* want to go.

### INSIDE STORY
## Close Encounters

Find out what it takes to make an aquarium shark feel at home. Picture yourself alongside scientists who spend 17 hours underwater in a small sub to learn about deep-sea creatures. Relive the excitement as one shark expert identifies a totally new species! The INSIDE STORY feature introduces you to men and women who've devoted their lives to studying sharks. You'll also meet people who have come face to face with these incredible animals – and have lived to tell their tales.

### HANDS ON
## Things to Do

Create a vacuum with a rubber suction cup and discover first hand how a remora stays attached to a shark. Use make-up to help you fade into the background just like a carpetshark. Check out other underwater creatures for yourself – in person. The HANDS ON features offer experiments and projects – practical ways to help you appreciate the special requirements of a shark's underwater world.

## Word Builders

What a strange word! What does it mean? Where did it come from? Find out by reading **Word Builders**.

## That's Amazing!

Awesome facts, amazing records, fascinating figures – you'll find them all in **That's Amazing!**

## Pathfinder

Use the **Pathfinder** section to find your way from one subject to another. It's all up to you.

Ready! Steady!
Start exploring!

# Introducing...
# Sharks

THERE IS MORE to sharks than the toothy jaws you've seen coming at you in the cinema or on television. And now's your chance to get a glimpse of a few of the different sharks that exist. First we'll meet sharks' ancestors, and then we'll cruise the deep alongside modern-day sharks. There are sharks with strangely shaped heads and others with tremendous tails. Some – the largest ones – have lost the need for teeth altogether. It's time to take the plunge...

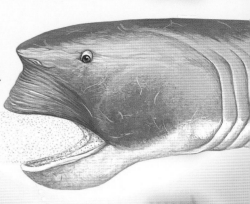

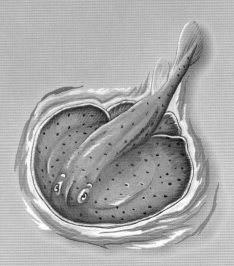

# What Is a Shark?

WHAT IS IT about sharks that terrifies people? Is it the gaping mouth, the jagged teeth or the cold eyes? Most people think of sharks as gigantic underwater monsters that attack people. But the truth is that most sharks are not dangerous to humans.

Sharks are fish, and like all fish, they have a strong, sturdy skeleton. What sets sharks apart from other fish is that their skeletons are made of a light, flexible, durable substance called cartilage, instead of bone. Sharks are known as cartilaginous fish.

Scientists have identified about 340 species of shark. All have a powerful tail, or caudal fin, and two sets of paired side fins. The pair towards the front of the body are called pectorals. The two towards the back are called pelvic fins. Most shark species also have two dorsal fins on their back and an anal fin on their underside near their tail. All sharks have at least five pairs of gill openings and gills, which absorb oxygen from the water.

All sharks are meat-eaters. Some eat prey as large as seals and dolphins. Others eat smaller sharks and fish. A few – the biggest of them all – feed on tiny marine creatures, such as plankton, shrimps and small fish.

Coral cod

## INSIDE STORY

### Seeing Sharks

Keeping sharks in aquariums is a tricky business. Many species will not even survive a trip to an aquarium because they simply cannot get enough oxygen in a small tank. Those that can make the journey present aquarists with other problems. They need an environment that mimics their native habitat, plus special shark-friendly tanks. Because sharks tend to rub against walls and bump into corners, aquarists try to build tanks that have smooth walls and no right angles. The walls of the tanks also need to be free of electric cables, because sharks are sensitive to electricity and will knock against the walls in search of the current. But aquarists are determined to overcome these problems. That way, we can observe, learn about and protect all sharks – both in aquariums and in the wild.

## FILTER-FEEDERS

Some sharks don't need teeth to eat. Instead, they suck in huge mouthfuls of water containing tiny animals and small fishes. They use comb-like sieves near their gills to strain the food from the water. A strong tongue flushes water across the gills, and out through the gill slits.

## SHOWCASE OF SHARKS

Not all sharks look alike. Some have flattened heads and wide, gaping mouths. Others have snouts like saw blades, or barbels on their chins. Sharks vary in size, too – some could fit into the palm of your hand, and others are bigger than a school bus.

Whale shark

## Word Builders

• The Latin word for meat or flesh – *carn* – gives us **carnivorous,** meaning 'meat-eating'. All sharks are carnivorous animals. Their food ranges from tiny plankton to large dolphins.
• A **barbel** is a spine or bristle that hangs from a fish's jaw. The word comes from the Latin *barba*, meaning 'beard'.
• **Crustaceans** are animals like crabs and lobsters that have hard external skeletons. The word comes from the Latin *crusta*, meaning 'shell'.

## That's Amazing!

Scientists are still finding new species of sharks. The megamouth – a shark as big as a large car – was first seen in 1976, when one was caught accidentally in a fishing net in deep waters off Hawaii. A filter-feeder that lives far away from the coast, the megamouth is still rarely sighted by divers. There is no telling how many unidentified sharks cruise the murky depths – waiting to be discovered.

## Pathfinder

• What were ancient sharks like, and how closely do they resemble the sharks of today? See pages 10–11.
• Rays and skates are related to sharks. Read about their similarities and differences on pages 24–25.
• Sharks have special adaptations that suit them to life under water. Find out more on pages 28–29.

## TAKING ITS TIME

The large Greenland shark is an example of how well sharks adapt to extremes in temperature. Seen here amid ice floes in the Atlantic, this shark moves slowly because of the cold, but it can catch fast prey such as seals. Scientists are not sure how it does this. They think it might have to do with small crustaceans that live on the shark – they glow in the dark and might attract prey.

Blue shark

## PREDATOR PREDICAMENT

To be successful hunters, or predators, sharks must find food, or prey, and then catch it. Smaller sharks have to worry about becoming prey for larger sharks, dolphins and killer whales. Sharks are extremely well equipped to meet these challenges. They have excellent sensory systems that let them pinpoint prey, as well as powerful muscles and streamlined fins that allow them to accelerate quickly.

## SILKY SKINNED

The streamlined silky shark fits everyone's idea of the perfect shark – smooth and graceful as it cruises through the sea. Silkies, so called for their smooth skins, live in warm waters all over the world, from 18 to 500 metres (60–1,640 ft) deep. They grow to nearly 2.4 metres (8 ft) long.

## FLAT SHARKS

Angel sharks are adapted for living, hiding and feeding on the seabed. Their speckled skin blends with their sandy home. They look like rays, but rays have gill slits on their undersides instead of on their sides. Named because their pectoral fins look like angels' wings, angel sharks are also known as monk sharks because their heads look like monks' hoods.

Angel shark

## NOSING AROUND

Sawsharks drag their barbels – sensitive 'whiskers' under their noses – through the sand to locate buried prey. Then they dig up the food with their long, tooth-studded snouts.

Sawshark

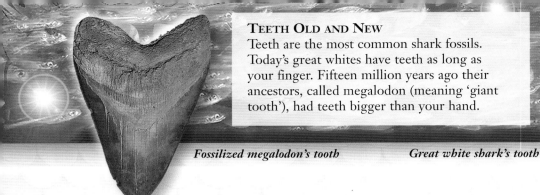

# The Ancient Ones

WITHOUT FOSSILS, WE wouldn't know much about Earth's past. Fossils are the remains of plants and animals – either impressions left in rock, or mineralized bones or teeth – that lived millions of years ago. Scientists called stratigraphers study the layers of rock that have formed throughout Earth's history, and palaeontologists study the fossils the rocks contain. Together they can piece together a portrait of life on Earth before we were around to see it all happen.

The most numerous and easy-to-find fossils are shark teeth. Millions of sharks over millions of years have shed millions of teeth. Other trace fossils – impressions of fins and bones – fill in the record on sharks. From these, scientists have worked out that ancient seas were populated with fierce predatory fish. The ancestors of sharks had cartilaginous skeletons, razor-sharp teeth and denticles – tooth-like scales covering their skin – just as modern sharks do.

The oldest shark-like fossils are found in rock layers formed about 400 million years ago. The first modern shark fossils, close relatives of living sharks, date back only 50 million years. Since then, sharks have changed very little.

*CLADOSELACHE*
This shark ancestor lived during the Devonian Period (see below). It was about 90 centimetres (3 ft) long. Its tail, or caudal fin, was like that of today's fast-swimming mako sharks – an almost symmetrical crescent.

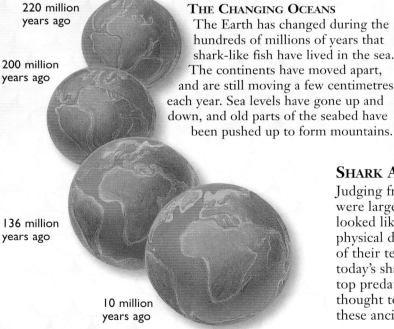

220 million years ago

200 million years ago

136 million years ago

10 million years ago

### THE CHANGING OCEANS
The Earth has changed during the hundreds of millions of years that shark-like fish have lived in the sea. The continents have moved apart, and are still moving a few centimetres each year. Sea levels have gone up and down, and old parts of the seabed have been pushed up to form mountains.

### SHARK ANCESTORS
Judging from the fossil evidence, there were large fish in ancient times that looked like modern sharks. Despite some physical differences, the size and shape of their teeth suggest that they, like today's sharks, were some of the sea's top predators. Modern sharks are thought to have descended from these ancient fish.

### SHARKS IN TIME
Earth's geological history is divided into Eras and Periods, which describe the age of rocks and fossils. The earliest shark-like fossils are found in rocks that formed in the Devonian Period. The shark species we see today appeared millions of years later in the Cenozoic Era.

| | Cambrian Period | Ordovician Period | Silurian Period | Devonian Perio |
|---|---|---|---|---|
| Pre-Cambrian Period | | | | |
| | | | | Palaeozoic Era |
| 4,600 million years ago | 550 mya | 505 mya | 435 mya | 408 mya |

## Word Builders

- **Palaeontology**, the word for the study of fossils and ancient life, is from the Greek words *paleo*, meaning 'ancient', and *-logos*, meaning 'word'.
- **Devonian** fossils were first found in ancient rocks near Devon, England.
- **Stratigraphy** comes from the Latin *stratum*, meaning 'layer', and the Greek *graphein*, meaning 'to write'.

## That's Amazing!

The fossil record of sharks goes back almost 400 million years, making it three times as long as that of the dinosaurs and almost 100 times longer than that of humans. Horn sharks have the longest fossil record of any living shark. The skeleton and teeth of a 160-million-year-old fossil shark look almost exactly like those of a horn shark you could see today.

## Pathfinder

- Is the megalodon's descendant, the great white shark, really as scary as people think? Turn to pages 14–15.
- Does the shape of a shark's tail affect how fast it swims? Find out on pages 20–21.
- Which modern shark resembles 200-million-year-old fossils? See page 54.

## HYBODONTS

These shark ancestors shared lakes, rivers and the seas with dinosaurs and other creatures. They all died out at about the same time – 65 million years ago. Hybodont remains have been found at dinosaur fossil sites in Wyoming, U.S.A. They grew up to 2 metres (6.5 ft) long.

## XENACANTHIDS

Remains of this mostly freshwater fish have been found all over the world. Xenacanthids evolved from *Cladoselache* and lived from Devonian to Triassic times. They were about 3 metres (10 ft) long.

## QUITE A STRETCH

Megalodon was an ancestor of the great white shark. Only fossils of its teeth have been found. From these, people have been able to make models of its jaws. Some of these models are probably far too big, but they still give a good idea of just how huge this shark might have been.

---

### INSIDE STORY

# Detective Work

Shark ancestors swam in the sea for millions of years. Suddenly they were gone. What happened? Scientists think that about 65 million years ago a meteor slammed into Earth. Fires raged, and the sky turned black. Some creatures, such as the dinosaurs and shark ancestors, may have died out as a result. We know something about the fish that perished from fossils. Most fossils are the hard parts of animals, because these last longer. Since sharks and their ancestors had few hard parts, complete fossilized skeletons are rare. The best fossils were formed when dead fish were buried quickly by silt in calm water. Scientists can then sometimes tell what fish ate from their fossilized stomach contents.

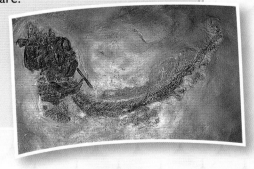

| | | | | | | |
|---|---|---|---|---|---|---|
|  |  |  |  |  |  |  |
| Carboniferous Period | Permian Period | Triassic Period | Jurassic Period | Cretaceous Period | Tertiary Period | Quaternary Period |
| | | Mesozoic Era | | | Cenozoic Era | |
| 360 mya | 286 mya | 248 mya | 208 mya | 144 mya | 65 mya | 2 mya | 0 |

# Putting Sharks in Order

EVERYONE HAS A family. Your immediate family includes your parents and brothers and sisters. Your other relatives – cousins, aunts, uncles and grandparents – make up your extended family. Sharks are divided into large, extended family groups, too. Scientists call these groups orders. The sharks in one order share certain features, and have all descended from a single ancestor.

There are eight orders of sharks. Scientists decide in which order to place a shark according to certain features, such as how many fins and gills it has, the location of its mouth or the shape of its body, fins and snout.

Sharks in two of the orders – the Lamniformes and the Carcharhiniformes – have many features in common. They have an anal fin, five pairs of gill slits, two dorsal fins, no fin spines and a mouth set behind their eyes. What sets them apart is eyelids. Lamniformes, including great whites and threshers, have none. Carcharhiniformes, including hammerheads and tiger sharks, have eyelids, so they can open and shut their eyes much as we do.

**NICTITATING EYELID**
All Carcharhiniformes, such as this oceanic whitetip, have a feature called a nictitating membrane – an eyelid that stretches, from bottom to top, over the eyeball and protects it. This is especially handy when the shark is eating a struggling fish that could poke and blind it.

Coastal sharks, such as the lemon shark, hunt for rays and bony fish near the sunlit surface.

The oceanic whitetip hunts far from the coast, in open sea. It eats fish, birds and turtles.

## INSIDE STORY
### Adaptation Wins the Day

When more than one kind of shark competes for the same food in the same place at the same time, some species will lose out. In order to survive, those species must change their habits in some way. Gradually, over many generations, a species may change its diet, or begin to feed at a different time. For example, many sharks eat fish. To avoid competition, some sharks have changed to eating hard-shelled creatures instead of fish. This nurse shark is munching on a lobster – its teeth have become specially suited for crunching. A change like this is called adaptation.

**FITTING IN**
Over many generations, a species changes to suit life in a special place. Great white sharks have adapted to live in cool waters, where seals and sea lions raise their young. Bramble sharks have adapted to become suction feeders of crabs and squids near the seabed.

### OUTWARD APPEARANCE

When trying to identify a shark, take a look at its physical features. Is the head conical, flattened or blunt-nosed? Where is the mouth positioned? How many pairs of gill slits are there? How many dorsal fins are there? Are they the same size?

**COUNT THOSE GILLS**
All sharks have at least five pairs of gills. Some sharks have six, like this bluntnose sixgill shark, or even seven pairs. Bony fish have several pairs of gills, too, but they are all protected by a bony cover with a single gill slit. Shark gill slits have no protection. Water comes out of the gill slits, taking with it dissolved waste products that the shark produces as it breathes and eats.

### Word Builders

• *Nictitare* means 'to wink' in Latin, so **nictitating** is a good name for a protective eyelid.
• Scientists have agreed that all names for shark orders will end in **formes**, from the Latin *forma*, meaning 'shape' or 'form'. Horn sharks, with their differently shaped teeth, belong to the order Heterodontiformes – *hetero* is Greek for 'other' or 'different', and *dont* is Greek for 'tooth'.

### That's Amazing!

• All sharks, no matter which order they belong to, must become skilled at hunting down food. A young lemon shark needs 86,520 kilojoules (20,600 cal) every day just to maintain its body weight. A human adult male needs 10,500 kilojoules (2,500 cal).
• The so-called blind shark, a type of collared carpetshark, is not really blind. When it is taken from the water, it looks as if it has no pupils because it rotates its eyeballs backwards in fright.

### Pathfinder

• Sharks have gill slits on the sides of their head. Where do rays have theirs? Find out on pages 24–25.
• What is so important about gills? Learn more on pages 32–33.
• Which shark makes its own light, and why? See page 56.

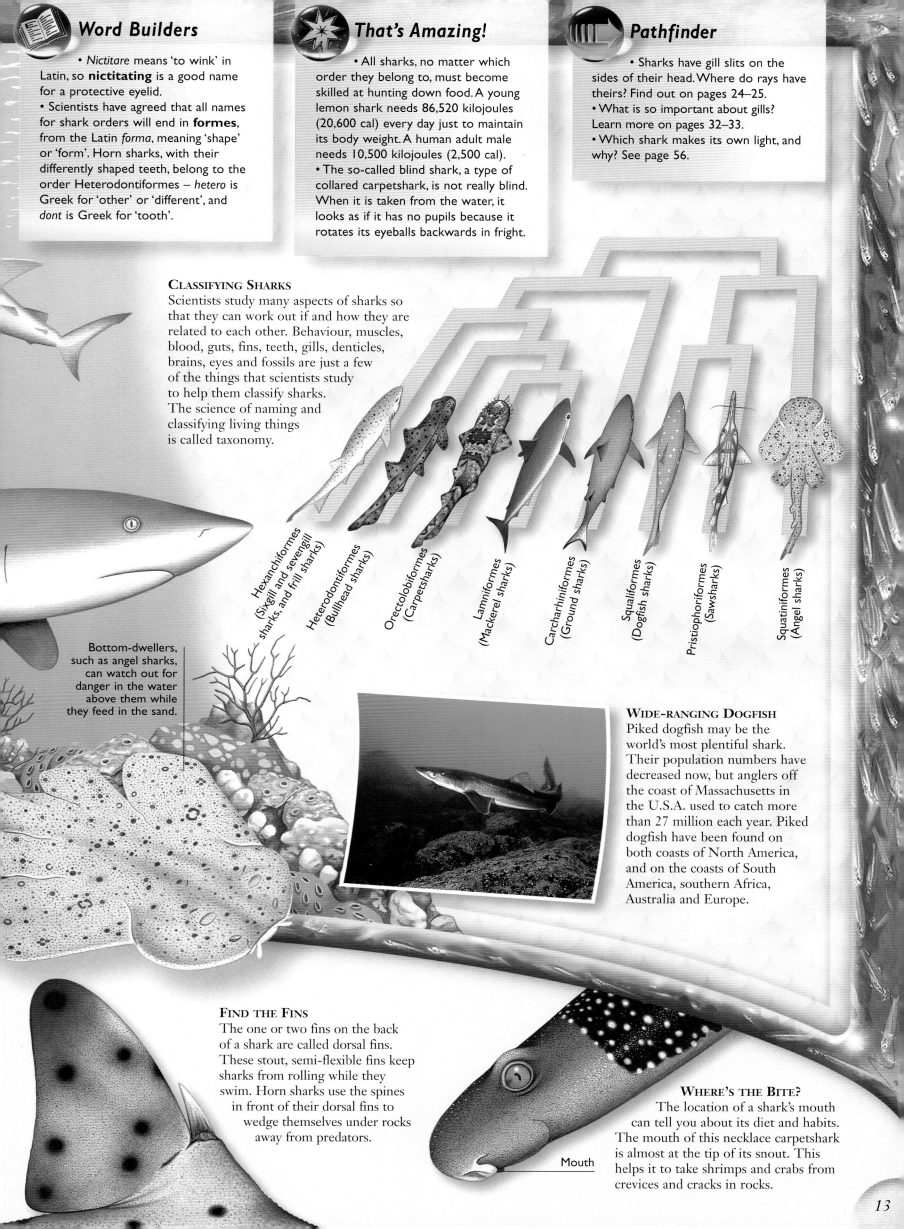

## CLASSIFYING SHARKS

Scientists study many aspects of sharks so that they can work out if and how they are related to each other. Behaviour, muscles, blood, guts, fins, teeth, gills, denticles, brains, eyes and fossils are just a few of the things that scientists study to help them classify sharks. The science of naming and classifying living things is called taxonomy.

Hexanchiformes (Sixgill and sevengill sharks, and frill sharks)

Heterodontiformes (Bullhead sharks)

Orectolobiformes (Carpetsharks)

Lamniformes (Mackerel sharks)

Carcharhiniformes (Ground sharks)

Squaliformes (Dogfish sharks)

Pristiophoriformes (Sawsharks)

Squatiniformes (Angel sharks)

Bottom-dwellers, such as angel sharks, can watch out for danger in the water above them while they feed in the sand.

## WIDE-RANGING DOGFISH

Piked dogfish may be the world's most plentiful shark. Their population numbers have decreased now, but anglers off the coast of Massachusetts in the U.S.A. used to catch more than 27 million each year. Piked dogfish have been found on both coasts of North America, and on the coasts of South America, southern Africa, Australia and Europe.

## FIND THE FINS

The one or two fins on the back of a shark are called dorsal fins. These stout, semi-flexible fins keep sharks from rolling while they swim. Horn sharks use the spines in front of their dorsal fins to wedge themselves under rocks away from predators.

Mouth

## WHERE'S THE BITE?

The location of a shark's mouth can tell you about its diet and habits. The mouth of this necklace carpetshark is almost at the tip of its snout. This helps it to take shrimps and crabs from crevices and cracks in rocks.

*Oceanic whitetip, 4 m (13 ft) long*

*Galápagos shark, 3.6 m (12 ft) long*

*Bull shark, 3.5 m (11 ft) long*

# The Heavyweights

IF YOU WERE to name one species of shark, it would probably be the great white. This is the shark that people think of first and fear most.

But the great white is just one of several formidable shark predators. The bull shark, the tiger shark, the mako shark and the Caribbean reef shark are all powerful animals with a taste for large, and often fast-swimming, prey. While these big hunters come from different shark orders, they do have certain similarities. They all have long, torpedo-shaped bodies that are sturdily built and widest at the front. This shape enables them to cruise for long periods in search of prey, such as squid, dolphins, seals and tuna. In fact, the great white must swim constantly, in order to breathe. These hunters, especially the mako, are also each capable of short bursts of great speed. All these sharks are ocean-dwellers, but one – the bull shark – can swim in fresh water and has been seen far up the Amazon river.

Other sharks in this group include the oceanic whitetip, a large, open-water fish that will dominate other shark species competing for the same food, and the Galápagos shark. The Galápagos is one of the few big hunters that is known to ward off enemies with a special display of threatening postures.

**MY PLACE, NOT YOURS**
Like many powerful shark species, Caribbean reef sharks can be a danger to humans when they are provoked. The trick is to learn what provokes them. Caribbean reef sharks will attack to defend their territory, and get excited by spearfishing or the use of shark bait.

## INSIDE STORY

### The Bite Factor

All the big hunters have especially powerful jaws that are perfect for stopping large prey in their tracks. But just how powerful is a shark's bite? Scientists have estimated that a great white (left) can exert a bite pressure of 140.6 kilograms per square centimetre (2,000 lbs/sq in). To put it in perspective, compare this to other creatures. A big dog has a bite pressure of 84.4 kilograms per square centimetre (1,200 lbs/sq in) and an adult human has a bite pressure of 4.6 kilograms per square centimetre (65 lbs/sq in).

**MAN-EATER?**
The great white shark, which can grow to 7.3 metres (24 ft), is the sea's top predator. Only killer whales are stronger and more deadly. Contrary to popular belief, great white attacks on humans are relatively rare – possibly 12 incidents in 10 years. Some victims have actually survived. And when death does occur, it is generally due to blood loss – not from being eaten.

## Word Builders

- A shark that defends the area around it is called **territorial** – from the Latin *terra,* for 'land' or 'property'.
- Most great hunters have subtle skin patterns and coloration, but the mako is very distinctive, with a metallic blue top and a white underside. This shark is also known as the **bonito** shark. *Bonito* is Spanish for 'pretty'.

## That's Amazing!

A gruesome murder was solved in Australia after scientists who worked at an aquarium caught a tiger shark in Sydney harbour. A week after the shark went on display, it vomited a man's tattooed arm. Someone had cut off the man's arm with a saw. A newspaper article about this event helped police catch the man's killer.

## Pathfinder

- To catch fast prey, sharks need to be good swimmers. Find out how they swim on pages 34–35.
- Learn more about shark teeth on pages 36–37.
- Sharks are at more risk from us than we are from them. See pages 58–61.

## ATTACKS ON PEOPLE

The International Shark Attack File has details of more than 3,100 attacks over the past 500 years – but how dangerous are sharks to humans? Numbers of shark attacks are on the rise because more people are using the sea than ever before. But the chances of being attacked by a shark are still extremely remote. Millions of people use the sea every day, but worldwide, only about six people per year are killed by sharks. Contrast that with 100 deaths from lightning each year in North America alone.

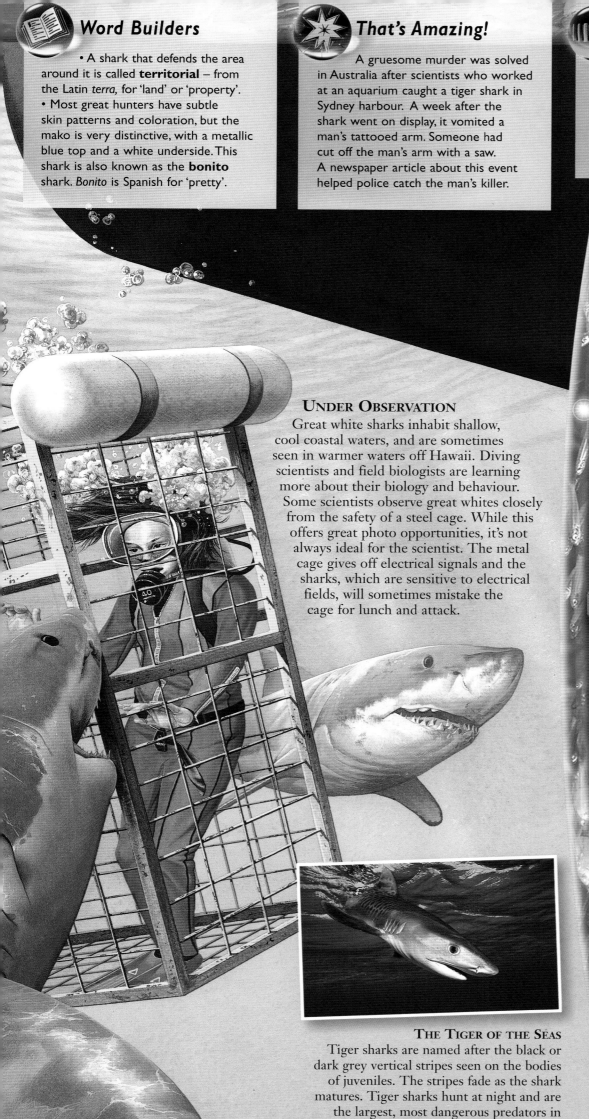

### UNDER OBSERVATION

Great white sharks inhabit shallow, cool coastal waters, and are sometimes seen in warmer waters off Hawaii. Diving scientists and field biologists are learning more about their biology and behaviour. Some scientists observe great whites closely from the safety of a steel cage. While this offers great photo opportunities, it's not always ideal for the scientist. The metal cage gives off electrical signals and the sharks, which are sensitive to electrical fields, will sometimes mistake the cage for lunch and attack.

6 per cent of attacks occur 150–300 m (500–1,000 ft) from the beach.

13 per cent of attacks occur 60–150 m (200–500 ft) from the beach.

51 per cent of attacks occur less than 60 m (200 ft) from the beach.

### ATTACK STATISTICS

Most people stay near the beach when they go swimming, so these statistics do not mean that it is safer to swim further from the beach.

### THE TIGER OF THE SEAS

Tiger sharks are named after the black or dark grey vertical stripes seen on the bodies of juveniles. The stripes fade as the shark matures. Tiger sharks hunt at night and are the largest, most dangerous predators in tropical waters. They grow as large as the great white, and live for up to 12 years.

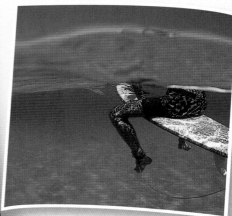

### SHARK'S EYE VIEW

Surfers are a relatively new and intriguing sight for sharks. We can't blame them if they think a surfer on a board might make a good meal, because their shape is a bit like like that of their usual diet of turtle or seal.

*Krill*

*Microscopic animal, or zooplankton*

# Huge but Harmless

YOU ARE SNORKELLING in warm, tropical waters when you see it. A giant shape looms before you, appearing suddenly out of the murk. It's a shark with a gaping mouth and a body the size of a school bus. You can actually see into its mouth and out through its gill slits. You and three friends could fit into the cavernous mouth. Are you next on the menu? No – this gentle giant is already getting its meal as it swims.

Swimming with its mouth open, the whale shark scoops and sucks up a living 'soup' of water, tiny plant and animal plankton, fish eggs and even small fish. Then it flushes the water through its gill slits before swallowing the strained food.

The whale shark, which can grow to 12 metres (40 ft) long, is one of three species of shark that filter their food from sea water. Basking sharks are slightly smaller filter-feeders that inhabit cooler waters to feed on plankton and shrimps. Like the whale shark, they are surface feeders. Megamouths are the smallest of the three, averaging about 4.5 metres (15 ft) in length. They feed on shrimps and small fish in deeper waters.

Whale sharks are related to wobbegongs, but basking sharks and megamouths are Lamniformes, which means that they belong to the same order as some of the most dangerous sharks, such as great whites and makos. So why aren't they predators like those sharks? Some scientists think that filter-feeding may be a primitive form of feeding that preceded the predatory ways of most modern sharks.

## BIG MOUTHS, LITTLE FOOD

A 9-metre (30-ft) fish needs a lot of food to survive, grow and reproduce, but contrary to popular belief, filter-feeders do not feed continuously. On average, they feed once or twice a week, but can go without food for weeks at a time if conditions demand it. To feed well, filter-feeding sharks need to find a place where there is a high density of food. Plankton is not found everywhere – only in concentrated groups that scientists call patches.

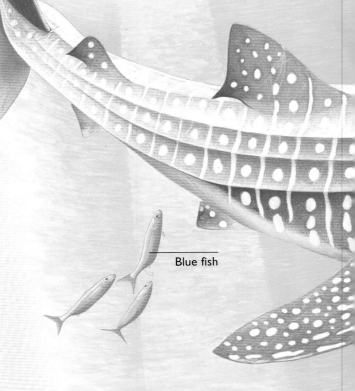

Blue fish

## INSIDE STORY
### Secrets of the Deep

Does the sea still hold mysteries? Are there any unidentified creatures swimming in the depths? Marine biologist Leighton Taylor is convinced the answer is yes. And based on his own experience, he is probably right.

In 1976, Dr Taylor was stunned to be the first person to recognize an entirely new kind of plankton-feeding shark, promptly nicknamed megamouth because of its large mouth. 'Finding a new species of plant or animal is not that rare. But this shark represented not just a new species, but also a completely unknown family of sharks. Finding something that different was a tremendous surprise. After studying it carefully, so that we could scientifically describe it, my colleagues and I decided it is related to the large group that includes makos, threshers, basking sharks and great whites.'

## MYSTERIOUS MEGAMOUTH

Since the first known specimen was discovered in 1976 in Hawaiian waters, just over 12 megamouths have been caught in waters near California, Japan, Brazil, Africa and Australia. Megamouths inhabit very deep waters, coming to the surface only at night. Perhaps that's why they are rarely seen.

Megamouth shark

## Word Builders

• *Densus* means 'thick' in Latin. A small volume of the ocean with a large number of shrimps has a high **density** of the creatures.
• In Greek, *mega* is 'very big'. The **megamouth** shark's huge mouth gives it both its common name, megamouth, and its scientific name – *Megachasma pelagios*, from the Greek for 'giant yawner of the open sea'.

## That's Amazing!

• Megamouth sharks have silver-coloured reflective surfaces inside their mouths. Scientists think these attract plankton and small fish, which then become the shark's dinner.
• Basking sharks that have shed their gill rakers can't eat. Scientists think these huge sharks may lie dormant on the ocean floor, living off fat stored in their livers, until the rakers grow back.

## Pathfinder

• Giant whale sharks have small relatives – wobbegongs. Read about them on page 23.
• Besides feeding, what else are gills used for? See pages 32–33.
• Whale sharks are as big as boats – and like boats, they carry passengers. Learn more on pages 48–49.

## MIGHTY MOUTHS

To get enough food, filter-feeding sharks must take in many litres of sea water. Each of the three species of filter-feeders does this in a different way. Even though they filter their food with gill rakers inside their mouths, these species still have teeth, just as other sharks do.

### A Varied Diet

Whale sharks eat mostly plankton and small fish, such as anchovies and sardines. But they can also swallow larger fish, such as mackerel and small tuna.

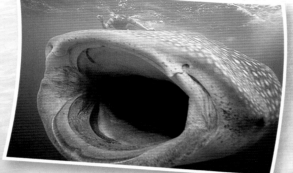

Whale shark

### WIDE MOUTH

Whale sharks have been seen in the middle of huge plankton patches, with their heads out of the water. When they sink beneath the surface, the food falls into their mouths. Then they rise back up, letting the water strain out through their gills, and start all over again.

### A Whale of a Journey

No one knows how far a whale shark swims in search of food. Scientists think that the whale sharks of Ningaloo Bay, Australia, may travel as far as 15,000 kilometres (9,000 mi) to waters off the coast of Indonesia.

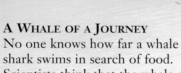

Plankton

### MOUTH LIKE A NET

The basking shark lifts its snout, lowers its chin and widens its jaws to make a huge net for plankton.

### HEAD LIKE A SIEVE

Basking sharks have the longest snout and the biggest gill slits of the three filter-feeding sharks. Like all filter-feeders, they travel over vast areas looking for dense patches of food. Basking sharks use their tooth-like gill rakers to sieve food from sea water. They may grow a new set every year.

*Filter-feeders accidentally take in microscopic plants, or phytoplankton, along with zooplankton*

### SCOOP MOUTH

The megamouth sticks out its upper jaw and drops its lower jaw to scoop up shrimps and plankton in mid-water.

# Head Hunters

YOU ARE SWIMMING through the water with a pair of hammer-shaped wings jutting from the sides of your face. Your eyes are set on the ends of these wings, so you have great side vision with which to track prey, but you can't see straight ahead because your eyes are too far apart. To compensate, you must swing your head back and forth to get a view of what's in front of you. The tiny sensory pores that every shark has are spread over the entire width of your broad head. That means you have a greater advantage in detecting the electricity emitted by creatures hidden in the sand or elsewhere in the dark waters. As you swim, propelled by sweeps of your tail, the wings on your face actually help to give you extra lift, especially when you move fast. Welcome to the world of the hammerhead shark.

There are nine species of these unusual-looking sharks. Their names give clues to their different shapes – scalloped, whitefin, smooth, small-eye and great hammerhead, plus the bonnethead, scalloped bonnethead, winghead and scoophead sharks. Although many sharks are loners, hammerheads are not. In fact, scientists are just beginning to realize how complex hammerhead behaviour and society really are.

## PINNED!

Although great hammerhead sharks prey on other sharks, skates and fish, they are particularly fond of stingrays. Stingrays feed on the seabed, and although they have eyes on the top of their heads, they don't always see an approaching shark in time to make their getaway. A great hammerhead can pounce quickly and pin a fleeing ray to the sand with the side of its head. Then it will turn and bite a chunk from the ray's wing as if it were a large, fleshy biscuit – one bite at a time until the ray is all gone. Divers must take care around great hammerheads – they are the only hammerhead known to attack people.

## IN THE SHALLOWS
The smooth hammerhead is the most widespread of the hammerhead sharks. It lives in shallow, warm inshore waters around the world – in North and South America, Hawaii, Africa, Europe, Asia, Australia and New Zealand. It hunts stingrays, skates, small sharks, sea bass and small fish such as herring and menhaden.

## SEEING SIDEWAYS
Hammerheads have a broader sideways range of vision than most sharks, but they are unable to see straight ahead.

## THAT'S USING YOUR HEAD!

As well as giving improved side vision, the wing shape of a hammerhead's head, or cephalofoil, offers several advantages. It helps the shark to swim by lifting it through water, just as wings give an aeroplane lift. In fact, some experimental planes have an extra pair of wings set far forwards like a hammerhead's. The shark also uses its head to help it to change direction – it tilts its head to one side in the same way as an aeroplane banks when turning. Hammerheads even use their heads to find prey, dig it up and hold it down.

## Word Builders

- **Cephalofoil** is the name that scientists give to the head shape of the hammerhead. This comes from the Greek word *kephalos,* for 'head', and the Latin word *foil,* for 'leaf' or 'thin sheet of metal', which refers to the flattened shape of the shark's head.
- **Hydrodynamics** – from the Greek word *hydor*, for 'water', and *dunamis*, for 'power' – is the study of the way things move through water.

## That's Amazing!

- The largest great hammerhead to be caught and measured was about 3 metres (10 ft) in length, but people have reported seeing much bigger ones of up to 6 metres (20 ft).
- Sometimes you really *are* what you eat. Take the small-eye hammerhead, also called the golden hammerhead. The small-eye gets its remarkable golden skin colour from a substance found in its favourite food – shrimps.

## Pathfinder

- How do sharks sense electrical currents in the water? Go to pages 30–31.
- Find out how other shark species and shark relatives are adapted for getting around on pages 34–35.
- Hammerheads often dig up buried food. What do other species do? Read more on pages 44–45.

**KEEPING AN EYE OUT**
Because the hammerhead's eyes grow on the two ends of a very wide head, this small-eye hammerhead would have seen the photographer only with its left eye. Its right eye saw something completely different.

**LOOKING FOR LUNCH**
Sharks have special pores on their heads that sense weak electric signals produced by their prey. Hammerheads like this bonnethead move their heads back and forth over the sand as they swim, to detect any signals given off by hidden animals. Bingo – lunchtime!

## INSIDE STORY

# Hammerhead Get-together

Underwater photographer Bob Cranston and film-maker Howard Hall have helped make famous the gatherings of scalloped hammerhead sharks in the Sea of Cortez off the Pacific coast of Mexico. Most sharks are solitary, but scalloped hammerheads form schools of up to 500 sharks, most of them female. Some scientists believe that the groups form to socialize and to avoid predators, but Cranston thinks the main reason is to mate. He has seen and filmed these sharks for himself: 'Occasionally a male would bite a female on the pectoral fin, and then wrap its tail around her and begin to mate. Then the two sharks would sink to the bottom. One time, a pair actually crashed to the seabed a short distance away from me.'

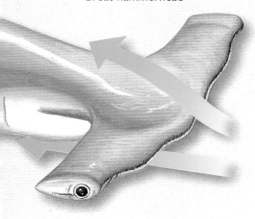

Great hammerhead

## HYDRODYNAMICS

As the hammerhead's tail pushes it forwards, water under the wing on its head rushes by at a slower rate than the water rushing over it. This lifts the shark's head and allows it to go faster with less effort.

## DIGGING UP DINNER

When a bonnethead's electrical sense finds buried prey, the shark converts its head from an electrical detection device to a shovel with which to dig out the food.

Bonnethead

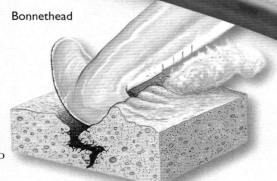

# Tall Tails

IF YOU THINK the tail is the safe end of the shark, think again. In thresher sharks, the tail is a lethal weapon – and a small fish's worst nightmare.

All thresher sharks have extremely long tails. They use them like whips to herd together the small schooling fish, such as mackerel and herring, that they like to eat. Most threshers swim the open waters, and once they've herded together their prey near the surface, the sharks cut and slash at the fish with their tails. This behaviour is called 'tail slapping', and the violent blows actually stun or even kill the prey. Threshers have even been seen using their tails to scoop food into their mouths.

Compared to bony fish, sharks don't have much diversity in the tail department. Since they are at or near the top of the food chain, most species use their tail for one purpose – powering forwards. The powerful swimmers have stiffened tails for maximum thrust through water. Ground-dwellers, such as nurse sharks and carpetsharks, have narrower tails with small lower lobes. The more flexible nature of these tails allows bottom-feeders to wriggle their way through cracks and over coral reefs as they hunt for food.

Yellowtail scad

### TURNING TAIL
The thresher shark has by far the longest tail of any shark. Threshers can grow to a total length of up to 6 metres (20 ft), and their whip-like tails are as long as the rest of their bodies. Long-line anglers sometimes pull up thresher sharks that have been snagged by the tail after they have tail slapped the baited hook.

### SPOTS AND STRIPES
Zebra sharks are so named because of the yellow and black stripes of the juveniles. As they mature, they develop a yellowish-brown colour with dark brown spots. These tropical reef hunters have tails almost as long as the rest of their bodies. They are sometimes seen resting on the seabed, propped up on their pectoral fins and facing into the current in order to get oxygen more easily from the water.

Upper lobe

### INSIDE STORY

## Surprise!

Skip Naftel, a fishing captain, helps biologists at the University of Hawaii by allowing them to study the sharks he catches. Students, who regularly join Naftel's fishing trips, are sometimes a source of entertainment for the captain and crew. Here, Naftel tells of a case of mistaken identity: 'One time, off Waikiki Beach, we pulled the line and it was obvious to me that we'd hooked a thresher by the tail. One student looked over the rail and said, "Wow, this shark has a weird head!" – not realizing he was looking at the tail. All of a sudden, the shark arched around. When the student saw the teeth coming, he shrieked and jumped back!'

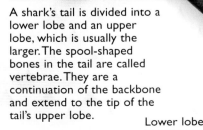

A shark's tail is divided into a lower lobe and an upper lobe, which is usually the larger. The spool-shaped bones in the tail are called vertebrae. They are a continuation of the backbone and extend to the tip of the tail's upper lobe.

Lower lobe

## Word Builders

• To **thresh** means to cut down grain crops, such as wheat, oats or barley, by slashing at them with a sharp blade. Thresher sharks strike at fish with their long tails in a similar way, which is how they got their name.
• **Diversity** means difference or variety. It comes from *diversus*, the Latin for 'turned in different directions'.

## That's Amazing!

Thresher sharks aren't the only sea creatures to use their tails for more than just swimming. Killer whales (orcas) hunt down fishes and kill them with powerful slaps of their tails. Great whites are also known to use tail slapping, though not to kill prey. Scientists think it may be one way that they communicate. Water is a good conductor of sound, so a loud tail slap might be heard miles away.

## Pathfinder

• Do ancient and modern sharks have similar tails? Find out on page 10.
• Some shark relatives defend themselves with poisonous spines on their tails. See pages 24–25.
• Learn more about how a shark swims on pages 34–35.

There may not be safety in numbers for schooling fish when a thresher shark is around.

## TELLING TAILS

The shape of a shark's tail can give you clues about how active it is. Symmetrical, crescent-shaped tails usually belong to sharks like makos and great whites, which need to swim fast because they hunt equally fast-moving prey. Long, low-set, thin tails generally belong to sluggish bottom-dwellers that feed on shellfish, crustaceans and other invertebrates.

### WE HAVE LIFT-OFF

As a shark swims it bends its body and tail from side to side as it moves forwards. The tail bends more than the body and produces forward thrust. Threshers gather so much momentum when they swim fast that they can jump right out of the water.

Paired pectoral fins help a shark steer by giving direction to the thrust of its tail. The pectorals on a thresher are longer than on most species. This may compensate for the powerful thrust from the extra-long tail.

Common thresher shark

Paired pelvic fins help stabilize a shark so that it doesn't roll from side to side.

**Nurse shark**
This shark swims with an eel-like motion, using its elongated tail to propel itself slowly in search of food.

**Tiger shark**
The long upper lobe helps this shark to twist and turn rapidly in pursuit of fast and agile prey.

**Mako shark**
Makos have flattened ridges called caudal keels at the base of their tails. These may reduce drag and help them to swim faster.

Caudal keel

*Graceful catshark, 60 cm (2 ft) long*

*Small spotted catshark, 90 cm (3 ft) long*

*Coral catshark, 60 cm (2 ft) long*

# Part of the Scenery

TO BE A successful predator, a shark must be fast enough to catch its lunch on a regular basis. But not all predatory sharks are fast swimmers. So what's a slow-moving yet hungry shark to do? It has to blend in with the background, and then ambush lunch. Many land and sea creatures, including some sharks, have colour patterns on their skin that allow them to blend in with their environments. This is called camouflage.

Sometimes an ambusher will try to look like something that its prey finds attractive. For instance, nurse sharks are known to curl their pectoral fins under to form a dark area in the water – the perfect hiding spot for small fish. When a fish swims in – lunchtime!

Camouflage can also protect a shark from becoming another shark's dinner. Newly born zebra bullhead sharks and tiger sharks have distinctive colour patterns that camouflage them from predators. As they get older, larger and better equipped to defend themselves, the patterns often disappear or change.

## ELEMENT OF SURPRISE

Even fast swimmers like this shortfin mako make good use of camouflage. Many sharks are counter-shaded – they have dark backs and light undersides, which allows them to blend in with the water around them when seen from above or below. They seem to swim out of nowhere to surprise their prey.

Tasselled wobbegong

Stonefish

## MASTERS OF DISGUISE

Camouflage is an adaptation, a combination of instinct and anatomy. Sharks are just one of many sea creatures that are able to camouflage themselves. An octopus, for example, can change its skin colour and pattern, and even texture, faster than you can blink. Stonefish can look just like rocks. This is dangerous for waders in the tropics because stonefish inject a deadly poison from their spines if stepped on. Flounders are able to create such a variety of colours that they can almost match a chessboard.

## Word Builders

- An **ambush** is an attack that surprises its victim because the attacker was hiding. It may come from the Latin word *imboscare*, meaning 'to hide in the bushes'.
- **Prey** is any animal that is hunted and eaten by another animal. It comes from the Latin word *prehendere*, which means 'to grab hold of'.

## That's Amazing!

- According to Hawaiian myth, sharks can camouflage themselves as 'shark men'. They trick swimmers by asking where they are going so that later, in shark form, they can find and attack them.
- Some bony fish have developed false eye-spots on their tails or the back of their fins, so that predators are tricked into attacking a part of the fish's body that is less vulnerable than the head.

## Pathfinder

- Wobbegongs are masters of ambush, but which sharks are speed kings? Find out on pages 14–15.
- What else besides camouflage protects young sharks from being eaten? Learn more on pages 42–43.
- Which shark uses its glowing belly to evade predators? See pages 56–57.

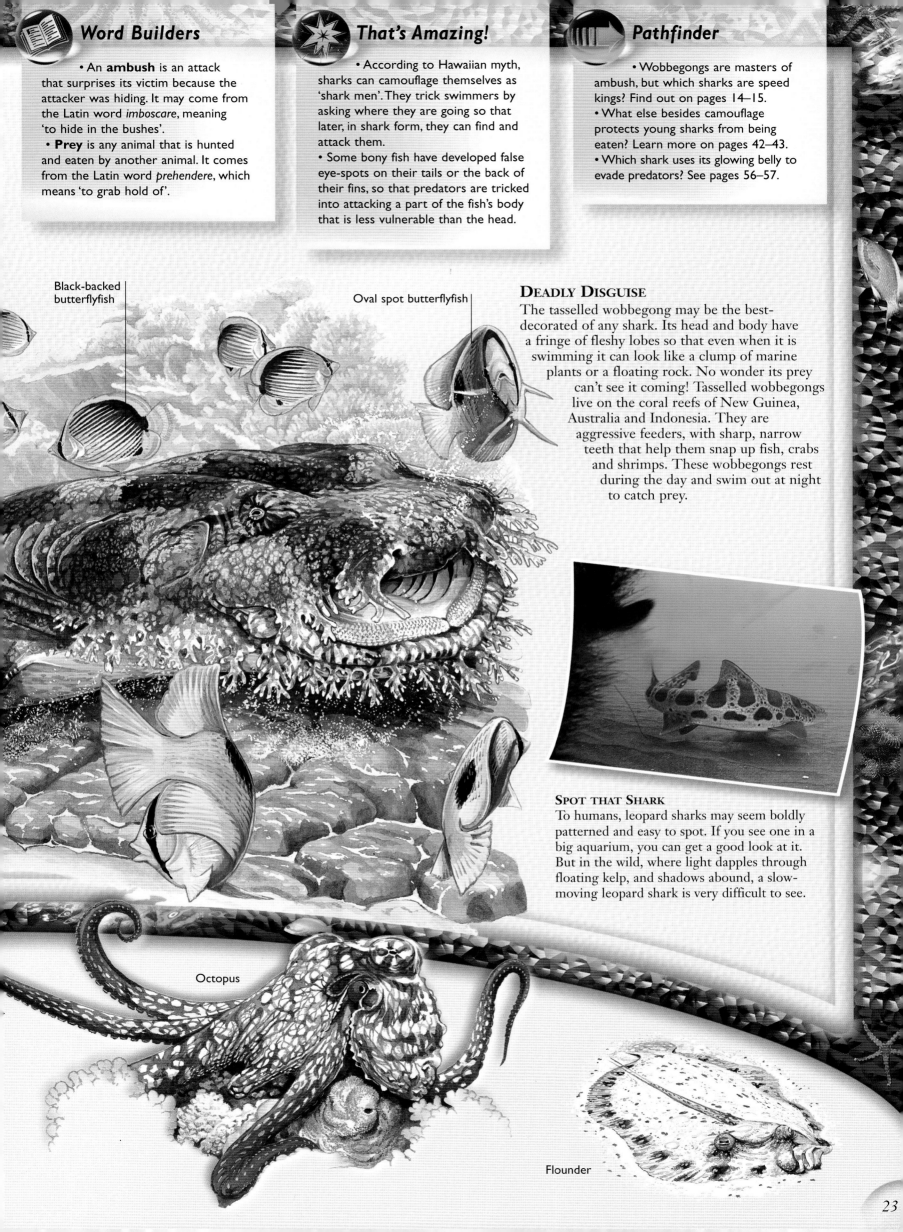

Black-backed butterflyfish

Oval spot butterflyfish

## DEADLY DISGUISE

The tasselled wobbegong may be the best-decorated of any shark. Its head and body have a fringe of fleshy lobes so that even when it is swimming it can look like a clump of marine plants or a floating rock. No wonder its prey can't see it coming! Tasselled wobbegongs live on the coral reefs of New Guinea, Australia and Indonesia. They are aggressive feeders, with sharp, narrow teeth that help them snap up fish, crabs and shrimps. These wobbegongs rest during the day and swim out at night to catch prey.

## SPOT THAT SHARK

To humans, leopard sharks may seem boldly patterned and easy to spot. If you see one in a big aquarium, you can get a good look at it. But in the wild, where light dapples through floating kelp, and shadows abound, a slow-moving leopard shark is very difficult to see.

Octopus

Flounder

23

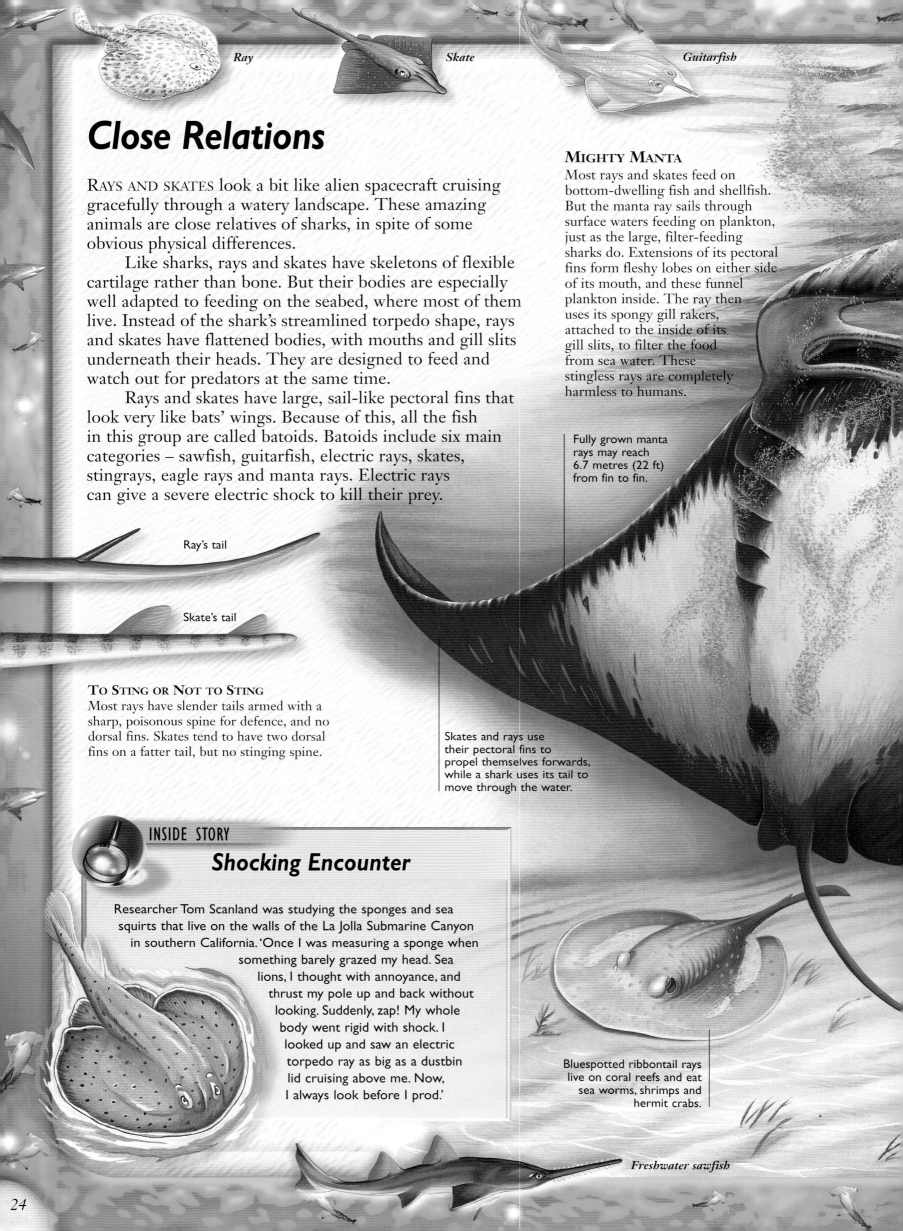

*Ray*  *Skate*  *Guitarfish*

# Close Relations

RAYS AND SKATES look a bit like alien spacecraft cruising gracefully through a watery landscape. These amazing animals are close relatives of sharks, in spite of some obvious physical differences.

Like sharks, rays and skates have skeletons of flexible cartilage rather than bone. But their bodies are especially well adapted to feeding on the seabed, where most of them live. Instead of the shark's streamlined torpedo shape, rays and skates have flattened bodies, with mouths and gill slits underneath their heads. They are designed to feed and watch out for predators at the same time.

Rays and skates have large, sail-like pectoral fins that look very like bats' wings. Because of this, all the fish in this group are called batoids. Batoids include six main categories – sawfish, guitarfish, electric rays, skates, stingrays, eagle rays and manta rays. Electric rays can give a severe electric shock to kill their prey.

Ray's tail

Skate's tail

### TO STING OR NOT TO STING
Most rays have slender tails armed with a sharp, poisonous spine for defence, and no dorsal fins. Skates tend to have two dorsal fins on a fatter tail, but no stinging spine.

### MIGHTY MANTA
Most rays and skates feed on bottom-dwelling fish and shellfish. But the manta ray sails through surface waters feeding on plankton, just as the large, filter-feeding sharks do. Extensions of its pectoral fins form fleshy lobes on either side of its mouth, and these funnel plankton inside. The ray then uses its spongy gill rakers, attached to the inside of its gill slits, to filter the food from sea water. These stingless rays are completely harmless to humans.

Fully grown manta rays may reach 6.7 metres (22 ft) from fin to fin.

Skates and rays use their pectoral fins to propel themselves forwards, while a shark uses its tail to move through the water.

### INSIDE STORY
## Shocking Encounter

Researcher Tom Scanland was studying the sponges and sea squirts that live on the walls of the La Jolla Submarine Canyon in southern California. 'Once I was measuring a sponge when something barely grazed my head. Sea lions, I thought with annoyance, and thrust my pole up and back without looking. Suddenly, zap! My whole body went rigid with shock. I looked up and saw an electric torpedo ray as big as a dustbin lid cruising above me. Now, I always look before I prod.'

Bluespotted ribbontail rays live on coral reefs and eat sea worms, shrimps and hermit crabs.

*Freshwater sawfish*

**Chimaeras** get their name from their strange appearance. In Greek mythology, the Chimera was a fire-breathing monster with a lion's head, a goat's body and a serpent's tail. These weird-looking shark relatives even have strange common names, including spookfish and ghostshark.

• Electric rays have special muscle cells in the centre of both pectoral fins that form a battery-like electric organ. An Atlantic torpedo ray can discharge 220 volts of electricity. That's about twice the voltage used in the average household – and enough to knock out a diver.
• The whitespotted guitarfish is known for its curiosity. It will prop itself up on the seabed, on the tips of its pectoral fins, just to get a better look at a diver.

• How old are the most ancient ancestors of today's sharks and rays? Find out on pages 10–11.
• There are six main groups of batoids. But how many groups, or orders, of sharks are there? Turn to pages 12–13.
• Not all rays swim in exactly the same way. Check out the differences on pages 34–35.

Fleshy lobes called celaphalic fins guide plankton into the ray's mouth.

Plankton is the collective word for tiny plants, crabs, shrimps, eggs, baby fish and the young of many sea animals that drift in currents.

### LOOPING THE LOOP
A manta ray can filter-feed constantly by looping through a cloud of plankton. If the manta swam straight through, it would waste time turning around in water that contained no food.

To breathe, a manta ray takes in water through its mouth, and expels it through gill slits, where its gills extract oxygen.

The height of a diver is just over one-fourth of the width of a very large manta ray.

Skates' fins are more pointed than those of rays.

### RIVER RAYS
Some ray species, such as the reticulated freshwater ray, live in rivers and lakes in South America, more than 1,610 kilometres (1,000 mi) from the sea. They stir the bottom with their pectoral fins to flush out the small creatures on which they feed.

## GHOSTS OF THE SEA

Sharks and rays have other, more distant relatives – the chimaeras. Although chimaeras share certain features with bony fish – they have a single gill opening on each side and a movable dorsal fin – scientists place them in the same group as sharks and rays. This is because, like sharks and rays, they have a skeleton of cartilage, they lack a swim bladder, and their eggs have tough, flexible cases.

**Family Ghost**
The shortnose chimaera is also known as a ghostshark or ratfish.

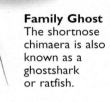

**Nosy Relation**
The spookfish has a long nose called a proboscis that has taste and touch sensors to help it find food.

**Digging for Dinner**
Also known as ploughnose, the elephantfish uses its nose to dig through the sand for food.

# Sharkworks

SHARKS LIVE IN an environment that we can only visit – water. Not only can sharks breathe underwater, but they can also hear and see in it. They can even 'feel' a possible meal swimming through it. Some shark species must swim constantly to survive, while others can lie still at rest. Still others have special coloration that helps them to hide from larger, faster sharks. What makes it possible for sharks to do all these things – and more? Read on and be amazed.

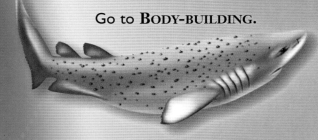

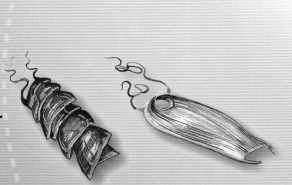

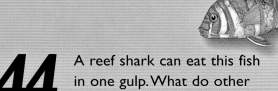

# Body-building

HUMANS HAVE BACKBONES. So do creatures like frogs, snakes and birds. Having a backbone, or vertebral column, is what distinguishes our group of creatures, called vertebrates, from invertebrates, which have no backbones. Insects, spiders and shellfish are all invertebrates. Having a backbone allows vertebrates to grow big because the strong, internal skeleton supports extra body weight.

Sharks, and all fish, are vertebrates. They have special adaptations, such as fins and gills, to suit them to life in water. Their fins and tails are designed for power, steering and balance in the water. The sleek shape and smooth skin of sharks allow them to cruise easily through the water, whatever their size. And a skeleton made of cartilage, which is lighter than bone, gives sharks great flexibility and speed while swimming. A few other vertebrates (see above) live a watery life, but all these must surface to breathe air. Of the vertebrates, only fish always breathe underwater. Their gills absorb oxygen from the water.

## INSIDE INFO

A shark's insides are a lot like ours. They have a stomach, intestine, liver, kidneys, pancreas, bladder and spleen. They also have a brain and a special case to protect it. But there are important differences. Most sharks have a special spiral-shaped valve near the end of their intestine. This shape provides increased surface area for digestion, without an increase in length. A shark's heart is tubular, while our hearts have chambers. And sharks don't have lungs. They have gills so that they can breathe underwater.

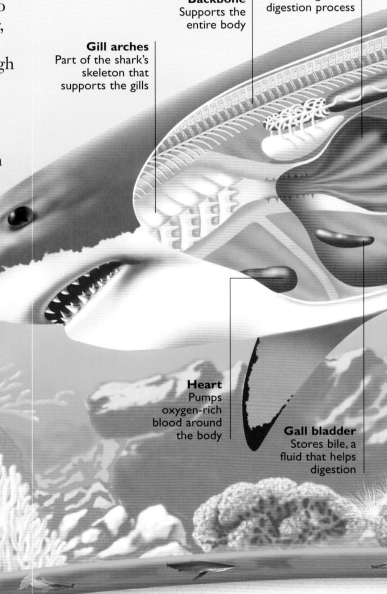

**Gill arches**
Part of the shark's skeleton that supports the gills

**Backbone**
Supports the entire body

**Stomach**
Begins the digestion process

**Heart**
Pumps oxygen-rich blood around the body

**Gall bladder**
Stores bile, a fluid that helps digestion

## TOOTHY SKIN
Bony fish have scales covering their bodies. Sharks have tooth-like denticles. These denticles have a hard enamel surface and many sharp ridges that reduce drag during swimming. Denticles act like armour, and protect the shark from injury.

## LARGE LIVERS
A shark has a large liver filled with fatty oils. Because these oils are lighter than water, the liver helps to keep the shark afloat. The oils provide a store of energy for the shark, too. With such large reserves, some sharks can go for months without eating.

A shark's liver can be 25 per cent of its body weight.

A healthy human's liver is 3 to 4 per cent of a person's total body weight.

## BORN TO SWIM

Sharks need large muscles to swim strongly and quickly. The muscles used for swimming can be 40 to 65 per cent of a shark's body weight. Other adaptations for swimming include a large liver and the ability to withstand tremendous water pressure.

## Word Builders

- **Denticles** are the tiny tooth-like things that cover a shark's skin. The word is from the Latin for 'little teeth'.
- We have a skull of bone to protect our brains. Sharks have a casing of cartilage, called a **neurocranium**. The word is from the Greek *neuron*, meaning 'nerve', and *kranion*, 'skull'.

## That's Amazing!

- The flesh of Greenland sharks often contains a strong neurotoxin – a chemical that stops nerves from functioning normally. Sleigh dogs that have eaten the raw meat of these sharks can't walk properly, and act as though they are drunk.
- Japanese samurai used shark and ray skin – complete with denticles – to make special grips for their swords.

## Pathfinder

- Denticles, like teeth, are hard enough to fossilize. You can read about fossils on pages 10–11.
- Which sharks use their tails to herd fish? Turn to pages 20–21.
- Now that you know how sharks digest their food, find out what they like to eat. Turn to pages 44–45.

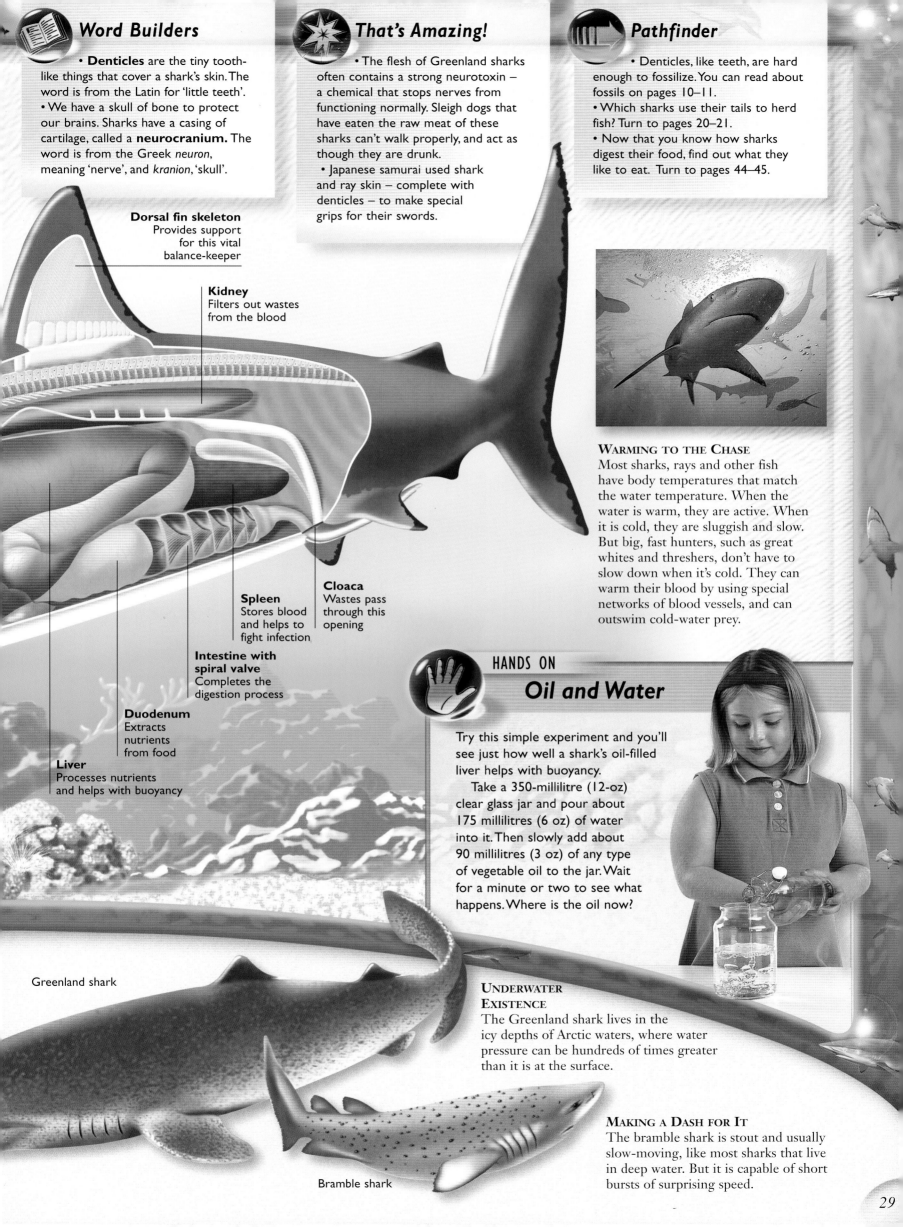

**Dorsal fin skeleton**
Provides support for this vital balance-keeper

**Kidney**
Filters out wastes from the blood

**Spleen**
Stores blood and helps to fight infection

**Cloaca**
Wastes pass through this opening

**Intestine with spiral valve**
Completes the digestion process

**Duodenum**
Extracts nutrients from food

**Liver**
Processes nutrients and helps with buoyancy

Greenland shark

Bramble shark

### WARMING TO THE CHASE

Most sharks, rays and other fish have body temperatures that match the water temperature. When the water is warm, they are active. When it is cold, they are sluggish and slow. But big, fast hunters, such as great whites and threshers, don't have to slow down when it's cold. They can warm their blood by using special networks of blood vessels, and can outswim cold-water prey.

### HANDS ON
## Oil and Water

Try this simple experiment and you'll see just how well a shark's oil-filled liver helps with buoyancy.

Take a 350-millilitre (12-oz) clear glass jar and pour about 175 millilitres (6 oz) of water into it. Then slowly add about 90 millilitres (3 oz) of any type of vegetable oil to the jar. Wait for a minute or two to see what happens. Where is the oil now?

### UNDERWATER EXISTENCE

The Greenland shark lives in the icy depths of Arctic waters, where water pressure can be hundreds of times greater than it is at the surface.

### MAKING A DASH FOR IT

The bramble shark is stout and usually slow-moving, like most sharks that live in deep water. But it is capable of short bursts of surprising speed.

# Talking Sense

ALL SHARKS ARE hunters – even the big filter-feeders. But in order to eat and survive, sharks must first find their prey. Since vision is limited underwater, sharks have developed a broad range of incredibly keen senses – all to help them find lunch.

Consider hearing. A shark can't hear sounds that a human takes for granted, but that's because it doesn't need to. Instead, its hearing is finely tuned to the low-frequency sounds that travel through water.

For example, a shark can hear the sound of a boat anchoring on a coral reef nearly two kilometres away. When a person on that boat hooks a fish, tiny drops of the fish's blood filter into the water. The shark can sense even a few molecules of blood and swims towards the scent. Pressure waves created while the shark swims bounce off obstacles, helping it to navigate quickly and accurately.

Nearing the boat, the shark can see flashes of the fish's silvery body as it struggles to free itself from the line. But as soon as the shark gets close to the fish, the fish disappears! The shark's eyes are too far apart to see what's right in front of it. But the special electricity-sensitive pores on its snout help the shark detect electrical impulses given off by the fish – and it closes in for the kill.

## THE EYES HAVE IT

Sharks have eyesight that's specially adapted for seeing in water. Generally, light enters the eye through the pupil and a lens focuses the light onto nerve cells at the back of the eye – the retina. Sharks have a special layer beneath the retina that reflects back some of this light, giving the best vision possible underwater. Many deep-sea sharks, such as the big-eye thresher, have especially large eyes to make the most of the available light.

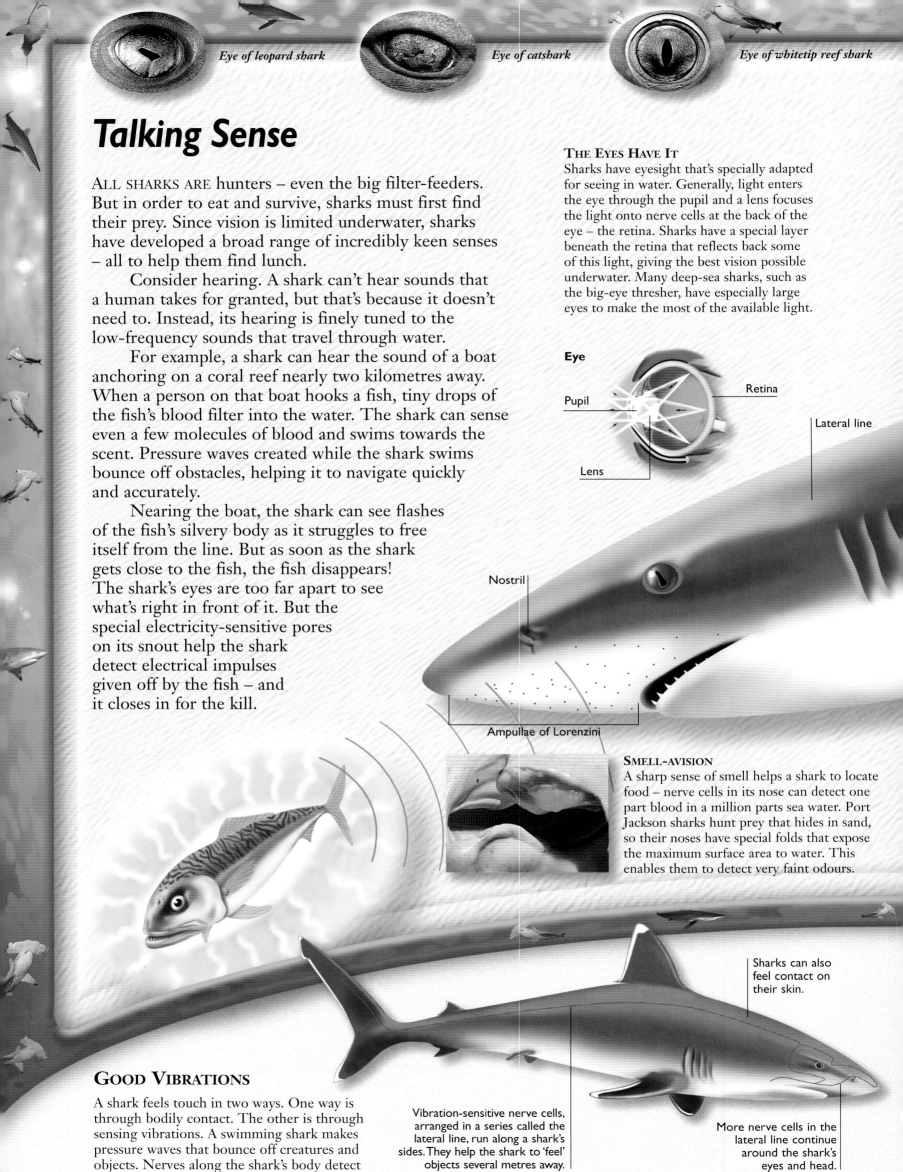

**Eye**

Pupil　Retina

Lens　Lateral line

Nostril

Ampullae of Lorenzini

## SMELL-AVISION

A sharp sense of smell helps a shark to locate food – nerve cells in its nose can detect one part blood in a million parts sea water. Port Jackson sharks hunt prey that hides in sand, so their noses have special folds that expose the maximum surface area to water. This enables them to detect very faint odours.

Sharks can also feel contact on their skin.

## GOOD VIBRATIONS

A shark feels touch in two ways. One way is through bodily contact. The other is through sensing vibrations. A swimming shark makes pressure waves that bounce off creatures and objects. Nerves along the shark's body detect the vibrations caused by the returning waves.

Vibration-sensitive nerve cells, arranged in a series called the lateral line, run along a shark's sides. They help the shark to 'feel' objects several metres away.

More nerve cells in the lateral line continue around the shark's eyes and head.

## Word Builders

- From the Latin word *rete*, meaning 'net', the **retina** is the layer of nerve cells at the back of the eye.
- **Lateral** means on the side of something – for example, the lateral line is on a shark's side. The word comes from *lateralis*, Latin for 'side'.
- *Ampullae* is Latin for 'small tubes'. The shark's **ampullae of Lorenzini** are tube-like sensory organs that detect weak electrical signals.

## That's Amazing!

- Ampullae of Lorenzini are named after Stefano Lorenzini, an Italian scientist who discovered them in the 1600s. It took another 300 years for experts to realize that these sensory organs detect electricity.
- The spiny lobster grinds parts of its shell together to communicate with other lobsters. Nearby tiger sharks have learned that this sound means lunch is just around the corner.

## Pathfinder

- When designing tanks for captive sharks, aquarists have to make allowance for their electro-sense systems. Find out why on page 8.
- How is a hammerhead shark's strange head shape related to its senses? Go to pages 18–19.
- There's no light in the deepest layers of the ocean, so some creatures make their own. See page 56.

## SCENT-SATIONAL!

For many years, people incorrectly called sharks 'swimming noses' because they thought they mainly used their sense of smell to find food. Now we know that, while they can smell very well, they are also able to detect electricity, see colours, sense distant vibrations and hear well through their watery environment.

Lateral line

Silvertip shark

## SWIMMER'S EARS

A shark looks as though it has no ears – all that is visible are tiny openings on the top of its head. Sharks actually have very sensitive hearing (even though the hearing is tuned to a different frequency than ours). A shark has inner ears inside its brain case, called macula neglecta. Fluid-filled tubes near the macula neglecta, called semicircular canals, regulate balance.

Skin

Macula neglecta

Semicircular canal

**Ear**

## INSIDE STORY

# How Smart Are Sharks?

When biologist Michelle Jeffries set out to test shark electro-sense, she also discovered how clever sharks can be. Her experiment involved two nurse sharks swimming in a Y-shaped maze. Each of the maze's two exits had a magnetic pole that was switched on and off at random. The sharks were given some food if they chose the exit with the active pole. But as the strength of the charge was reduced, it got harder for the sharks to sense it, and sometimes they would make mistakes. 'But they soon realized that this meant missing out on a treat,' said Jeffries. 'One time I even caught a shark clambering over the barrier into the other exit lane just to get at the food.'

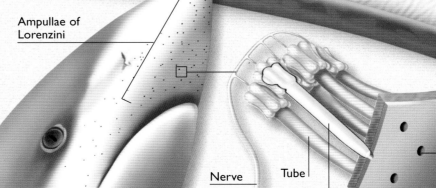

## THE BODY ELECTRIC

Sharks have an extra sense that humans don't have. They can detect electricity in sea water with a network of jelly-filled pores, called ampullae of Lorenzini, spread across their snouts. These pores help sharks to detect the weak electrical fields created by a fish when it moves. Hammerhead sharks, with their broad heads, have a long series of such cells. They can find prey in the sand and in crevices, and perhaps even navigate with the electrical signals they receive.

Ampullae of Lorenzini

Nerve

Tube

Jelly

Surface pore

**Close-up of ampullae of Lorenzini**

*Leopard shark
(a fivegill shark)*

*Bluntnose sixgill
(a sixgill shark)*

*Broadnose sevengill
(a sevengill shark)*

# Deep Breathing

TAKE A BREATH. There. When you're human, getting life-giving oxygen is that easy. Getting oxygen is quite simple for a shark, too, but it does it in a different way from you, because it has to breathe underwater.

Sharks need oxygen for survival, as all animals do. Inside the body's cells, oxygen combines with nutrients from food to create energy. Sharks and other fish have developed special organs called gills for getting oxygen from water. A shark breathes by taking in water through its mouth like we take in air. The water flows over the gills, which remove the oxygen, before passing out through the gill slits. When sharks swim, water is forced over the gills so they get oxygen. The faster they swim, the more oxygen they get. But not all sharks have to swim to breathe. Some bottom-dwellers have learned to pump water over their gills while keeping still.

The gills contain many blood vessels because blood carries oxygen from the gills to the rest of the body. Blood also carries wastes, such as carbon dioxide, from the cells to the gills, where they pass into the water.

### RAMMING IN OXYGEN
Large, fast-swimming sharks such as makos and great whites (above) need plenty of oxygen in order to push their muscles harder. This means they must force large volumes of water over their gills. By swimming fast with their mouths barely open, they can force oxygen-containing water over their gills. This process is called ram ventilation.

## BREATHING WITH GILLS
Sharks are not the only animals with gills. Most creatures that live in water use them. All fish have gills, as do octopus, squid, shrimps and all other shellfish. Most sharks have five pairs of gills, but two families – the sixgill and sevengill sharks – have more.

Caribbean reef shark

Gill opening

### HOLD STILL AND BREATHE
This scientist is using a special dye to study the flow of water through a nurse shark's gills. When at rest, these sharks use their gill and throat muscles to pump water over their gills.

## HOW GILLS WORK
Gills are a series of blood-filled structures in the shark's throat that help it to breathe in water. Each gill has hundreds of feathery gill filaments that are filled with oxygen-absorbing blood. Gill filaments are supported by part of the shark's skeleton called the gill arches. By swimming forwards and using throat muscles to pump, a shark pushes water over the gills and out through gill slits. Big arteries bring blood to the gills, and this blood gives the gills their red colour.

## Word Builders

- **Ventilation** comes from *ventus,* the Latin word for 'wind'.
- A **filament** is a very fine thread. The word comes from the Latin *filare,* meaning 'to spin'. Filaments are spun together to make thread.
- A **nutrient** is any substance that feeds an animal or plant. The word comes from the Latin *nutrire,* meaning 'to nourish'.

## That's Amazing!

- In just one hour of swimming, a basking shark may push more than 22,500 litres (6,000 gal) of sea water through its gills.
- A tagged shortfin mako shark swam 2,128 kilometres (1,322 mi) in 37 days – an average of 58 kilometres (36 mi) a day. If it swam at that speed for all of its 15-year life, it would swim about 320,000 kilometres (200,000 mi) – the equivalent of eight times around the world.

## Pathfinder

- What do gills have to do with eating? See pages 16–17.
- Tails are great for swimming. But in some sharks, the tail has other uses. Read more on pages 20–21.
- Which creatures use sharks' gills as a source of food? The answer is on pages 48–49.

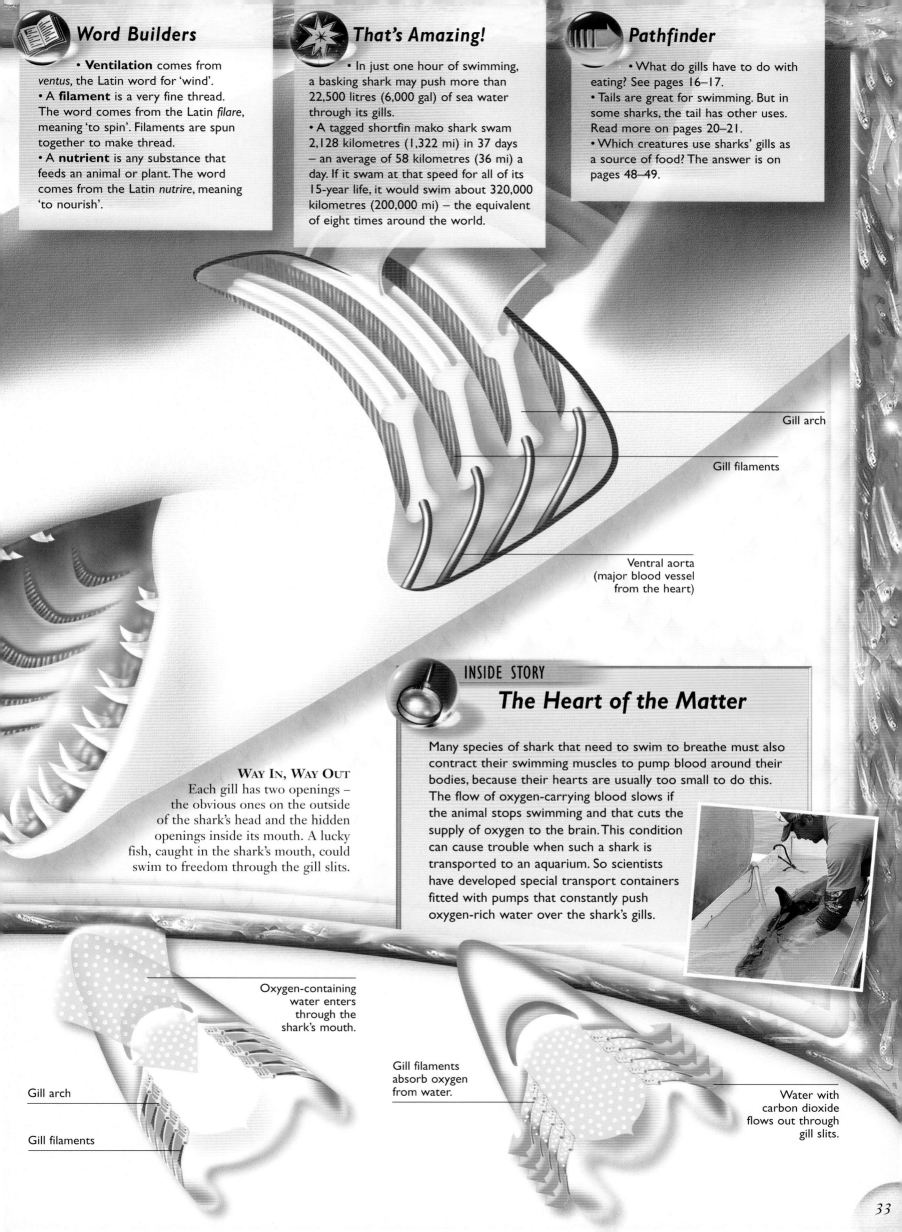

Gill arch

Gill filaments

Ventral aorta (major blood vessel from the heart)

### WAY IN, WAY OUT

Each gill has two openings – the obvious ones on the outside of the shark's head and the hidden openings inside its mouth. A lucky fish, caught in the shark's mouth, could swim to freedom through the gill slits.

### INSIDE STORY
# The Heart of the Matter

Many species of shark that need to swim to breathe must also contract their swimming muscles to pump blood around their bodies, because their hearts are usually too small to do this. The flow of oxygen-carrying blood slows if the animal stops swimming and that cuts the supply of oxygen to the brain. This condition can cause trouble when such a shark is transported to an aquarium. So scientists have developed special transport containers fitted with pumps that constantly push oxygen-rich water over the shark's gills.

Gill arch

Gill filaments

Oxygen-containing water enters through the shark's mouth.

Gill filaments absorb oxygen from water.

Water with carbon dioxide flows out through gill slits.

*The salmon shark is 3 metres (10 ft) long from nose to tail*

*The Atlantic devil ray has a 1.5-metre (5-foot) wingspan*

# Swimming Lessons

COMPARED TO FLYING in air, 'flying' in water is easy. Water is 800 times as heavy as air and holds up much more weight. But in many other ways swimming through water is like flying through air. Think of the shark's tail as an aeroplane propeller, but set at the back, and the pectoral fins as an aeroplane's wings and flaps. The power of the tail drives the shark forwards and the pectoral fins help the shark climb or dive.

If a broad, powerful tail is so important, how do skates and rays, which have slender, whip-like tails, manage to 'fly' through the water? These relatives of sharks get their power from their big pectoral fins. Some, such as manta rays and bat rays, swim along in open water, flapping their pectoral fins like wings, a bit like birds. Stingrays, however, do not flap their fins. They use their strong pectoral muscles to ripple along the bottom.

Birds can overcome gravity because they don't weigh much for their size. The same is true of sharks and their relatives. Cartilage is lighter than bone, and this allows even the largest cartilaginous fish to slice through the water with a minimum of effort. Large livers filled with fatty, lighter-than-water oils also make sharks buoyant.

Bat ray

**GOING INTO HIDING**
Well-developed pectorals are useful for more than just swimming. Rays and skates use their pectoral fins to cover themselves with sand in order to hide from predators.

Thornback ray

**DOUBLE WHAMMY**
When you see a swimming ray, you might think it has two faces. That's because it has eyes on its upperside and its mouth and gills on its underside, and both can be seen when the fish is on the move.

**HOW THEY SWIM**
Sharks and rays swim differently. Rays flap their pectoral fins as if they were flying. Sharks move their tails from side to side to push themselves forwards. A shark's pectoral fins merely control its direction.

## Word Builders

- **Buoyancy** is the ability to float. It comes from the Spanish word for 'float' – *boyar*.
- **Pectoral** fins are on either side of a fish, about where the chest might be. In Latin, the word *pector* means 'breast' or 'chest'.
- **Gravity** is the force that draws an object or living thing downwards. The word comes from the Latin *gravis*, meaning 'heavy'.

## That's Amazing!

- Shark babies can swim and hunt as soon as they are born. The great white shark swims non-stop for its entire life.
- One of the fastest-swimming sharks is the mako. It has a streamlined, torpedo-shaped body that is ideal for cruising and for sudden bursts of high speed. Speeds of 35 kilometres (22 mi) per hour have been recorded.

## Pathfinder

- Most sharks swim alone, but some hammerheads prefer company. Find out why on page 19.
- Different tails for different sharks? Learn more on pages 20–21.
- Swimming uses a lot of oxygen. How do sharks manage to breathe underwater? Find out on pages 32–33.

## WINGING IT

Stingrays and skates stay near the seabed, but eagle rays, cownose rays and manta rays seem to fly through the water, far above the bottom. Manta rays can be found a long way offshore, near the surface but in very deep water.

Blue shark

## ROCK CLIMBER

The nurse shark is a sluggish bottom-dweller that sometimes uses its specially adapted pectoral fins for clambering rather than swimming. The fins help it to move across the rocky seabed. The nurse shark doesn't need to swim to breathe – an ideal adaptation for a creature that is often seen resting on reefs and rocks.

## THEY GET AROUND

Some sharks can swim rapidly only for short distances, while other species have the stamina of marathon runners. Blue sharks caught, tagged and released off Massachusetts, U.S.A. were caught again near Spain 40 days and 3,220 kilometres (2,000 mi) later. Tag returns show that blue sharks regularly swim back and forth across the Atlantic Ocean. These trips require strong muscles, stamina and the ability to navigate. Just how sharks find their way is something scientists are still studying.

### INSIDE STORY

# The Problem with Pecs

All sharks have pectoral fins. These fins can bend and tilt to help the shark manoeuvre and brake. They also steady the shark's body as it swims. In many sharks, the pectoral fins are shaped like a shallow upside-down bowl, providing lift as the shark moves forwards. The size and shape of the pectorals vary between species. Those of the fastest sharks, such as the mako (see below), are short with a small surface area to reduce drag. They are also stiff, helping the shark to turn sharply at high speed. Other sharks, such as hammerheads, also have small pectorals that don't give much lift. However, the hammerheads' broad heads compensate for this, giving them that extra lift. Sluggish bottom-dwellers such as angel sharks don't need speed, so they've developed pectoral fins that are large and broad.

# The Cutting Edge

WHEN YOU THINK of sharks, you may automatically think of teeth. All sharks have teeth, even the big filter-feeders that do not use them. But for all their amazing teeth, there's one thing that sharks can't do – chew their food. While different sharks have developed specialized teeth for tackling different food items, the end result is the same: sharks use those teeth to cut food up into chunks small enough to swallow. If a shark swallows its food whole, it uses its teeth to hold or disable the prey.

Sharks usually have only one kind of tooth, depending on what they eat. Makos have stabbing teeth for grabbing hold of fast prey. Wobbegongs have small, sharp teeth for crushing shellfish. Great whites have slicing teeth for cutting large prey into smaller pieces. Horn sharks are an exception. They have both stabbing and crushing teeth – perfect for grabbing spiny sea urchins and crunching them up. This mixture of teeth is called heterodonty, and it gives this order of sharks – the Heterodontiformes – its name.

Although sharks can go through thousands of teeth in a lifetime, they generally have only one row, or band, of teeth in a biting position. As teeth are broken or wear out, new ones move up and out to take their place.

### NONE TOO SHARP

How did the gummy shark, a type of smooth dogfish, get its name? Without sharp teeth to slice up its food, this shark appears to gum it instead. Its flat teeth can crush bottom-dwelling creatures such as octopus, fish and shrimps.

### JUTTING JAWS

People used to think that sharks had to turn over to bite because their noses got in the way. Now we know that the shark has muscles that lift the snout up and out of the way. Protrusile jaws – jaws that can be pushed out and forwards then drawn back in again – increase the power of the shark's bite and let it grab relatively large prey easily.

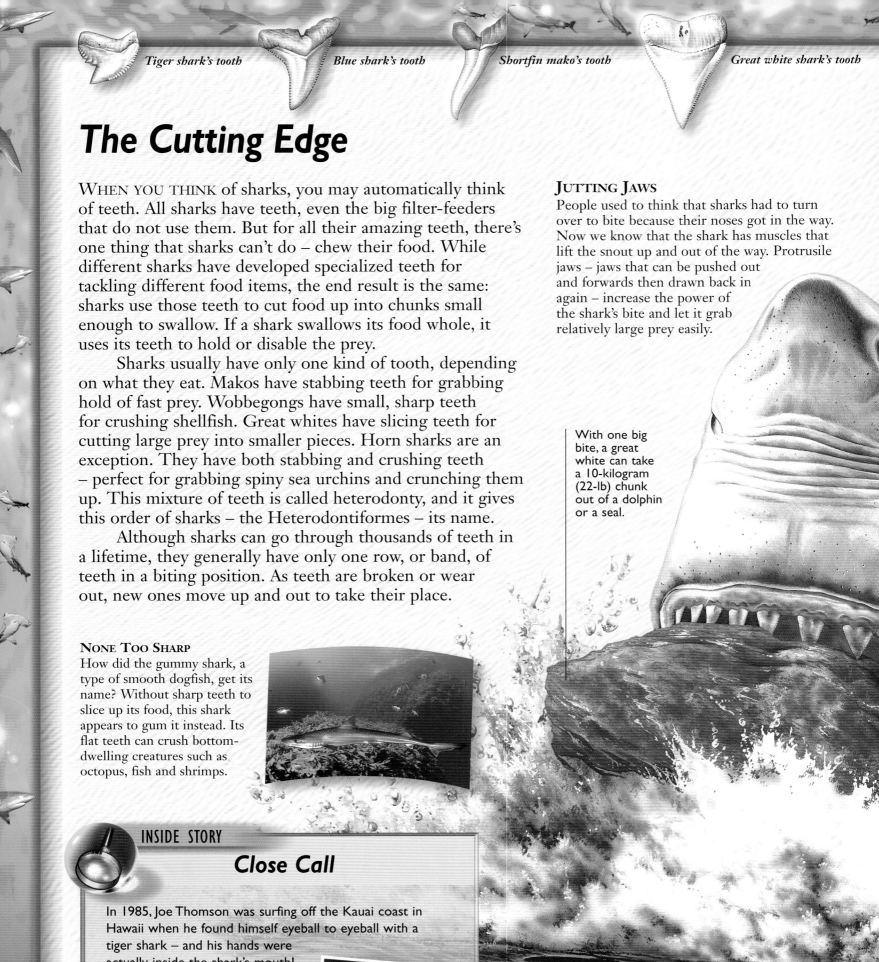

With one big bite, a great white can take a 10-kilogram (22-lb) chunk out of a dolphin or a seal.

---

**INSIDE STORY**

## Close Call

In 1985, Joe Thomson was surfing off the Kauai coast in Hawaii when he found himself eyeball to eyeball with a tiger shark – and his hands were actually inside the shark's mouth! He was able to free one hand, and repeatedly punched the shark in the eye until it released its grip. He managed to escape, but with only one of his hands. He made it to the beach and hitched a ride to a hospital. But he sent his friends back to retrieve the surfboard.

## Word Builders

- **Heterodonty** comes from the Greek words *hetero,* meaning 'other' or 'different', and *odon,* meaning 'teeth'.
- **Protrusile** comes from the Latin words *pro,* meaning 'in front of', and *trudere,* meaning 'to thrust'.

## That's Amazing!

- A shark may use more than 30,000 teeth in its lifetime. It can have up to 3,000 teeth in its mouth at once.
- In mediaeval times, sharks' teeth were used to detect poison in drinks. The brew was thought to be deadly if it fizzed when the tooth was dropped into the liquid.

## Pathfinder

- How big were the teeth and jaws of a megalodon, an extinct cousin of the great white? Find out on pages 10–11.
- How do tiny tooth-like structures, called denticles, on a shark's skin help it to swim fast? Go to page 28.
- Do sharks use their teeth during courtship? See pages 38–39.

### SAY 'AAAAH!'

A great white's powerful jaws are made of light and flexible cartilage. The two bumps on the top of this upper jaw show where it was loosely connected to the bottom of the shark's brain case, allowing the jaws to detach from the brain case when the shark attacked. The teeth in the back of the jaw are much smaller than the teeth in the front.

### OPEN WIDE

Jaws that slide out of the mouth sound like something out of a science fiction film. But slow-motion footage of feeding sharks confirms the truth. Protrusile jaws give the shark a better grip on its prey, and absorb some of the force of its powerful bite.

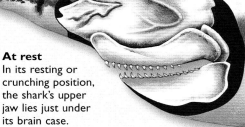

**At rest**
In its resting or crunching position, the shark's upper jaw lies just under its brain case.

**Jaw dropping**
The shark moves to grab its prey. Its snout lifts up, its upper jaw slides forwards, and its lower jaw drops.

### CONVEYER-BELT TEETH

A shark's teeth are always sharp. The rate of replacement is unknown for most species, but experiments with captive lemon sharks and horn sharks show that each tooth lasts from one month to about a year. The thousands of teeth lost during a shark's life fall to the seabed and may eventually become fossils.

**Extra bite**
Once the jaws are fully open, muscle contractions force the upper jaw away from the brain case and out of the shark's mouth.

*Mermaid's purse*        *Horn shark's egg case*

# Next Generation

HAVING BABIES IS the ultimate goal of all animals.
After all, producing young is vital for the survival
of any species, and sharks are no exception.

But sharks reproduce differently from most of the
sea creatures that surround them. Most marine animals
release sperm and eggs into the water at the same time,
and when sperm joins with an egg, fertilized eggs are
the result. With sharks, however, fertilization takes
place inside the female's body, just as in mammals.
Male sharks transfer sperm to the females with
organs called claspers.

Depending on the shark, fertilized eggs develop
in one of three ways. Some sharks lay egg cases
that attach to surfaces. Others keep their eggs
inside them, where pups develop and hatch
before being born into the water. Several
species bear live young without any
egg cases. These sharks have placentas with
umbilical cords that nourish the young as they
develop. It usually takes them six to twelve months
to produce their pups. Many shark population
numbers are low because people are catching
the sharks faster than they can reproduce.

**MALE VERSUS FEMALE**
All male sharks and rays have a pair
of claspers between their pelvic fins
for fertilizing the females' eggs.

### PRE-MATING BALLET
Before mating, a male and female shark swim
gracefully around each other like ballet dancers.
The male signals his intentions by nipping
his mate on her back. She stops swimming, and
together they spiral down towards the seabed.

### INSIDE STORY
## *Living Under Glass*

Scientists have learnt much about shark reproduction from
sharks that have given birth in large aquariums. One of the
world's most successful shark breeders is Senzu Uchida of
the Okinawa Expo Aquarium in Japan. He was the first
person to catch and display the world's largest fish – the
whale shark. In a 3,785,000-litre (one-
million-gal) tank, Uchida has studied
mothers and pups of seven kinds of ray
and seven kinds of shark, including
whitetip and blacktip reef sharks, and bull
sharks. Uchida says, 'We have to be
careful about including bull sharks in
displays. They will eat pups, mantas and
even tiger sharks. If bull sharks are
included, they must be fed all the time.'

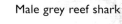
Male grey reef shark

### Word Builders

• The **placenta** is a flattened, spongy organ inside a pregnant animal. The word comes from the Greek for 'flat cake' – *plakoeis*. The placenta nourishes the baby, which is attached to it by the umbilical cord.
• *Umbilicus* is Latin for 'navel' or 'centre'. The **umbilical cord** is a tube running from the foetus' navel (belly-button) to the placenta.

### That's Amazing!

• Expectant shark mothers lose their appetite just before giving birth. And a good thing, too – it stops them from eating their own babies.
• Newborn spined pygmy sharks are less than 12 mm (½ inch) long. Contrast that with newborn basking sharks, which are 170 cm (66 inches) long – as big as an adult human.

### Pathfinder

• How fast does a shark pup grow? And how do we know how old a shark is? Turn to pages 40–41.
• Why do pregnant grey reef sharks congregate in warmer waters? The answer is on page 51.

## HIDING HER EGGS

Once mother sharks have laid their eggs, they do not stay around to protect them. However, they do make sure that the egg cases – each containing one baby and one nourishing yolk – rest in a safe place. It may take up to 24 months for a pup to hatch. Shark egg cases have flexible brown covers. They are not fragile like birds' eggshells.

### ONCE BITTEN

A quick look at a female shark's back and pectoral fins can confirm whether she's mated. Scars on her back and pectoral fins show that a male has bitten her during mating. A lack of scars suggests she has not yet begun courtship.

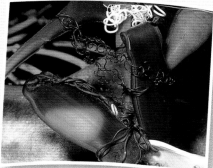

### ANCHORING AN EGG

Swellsharks, catsharks and dogfish lay flat, rectangular egg cases called mermaids' purses. All four corners have hooks or long threads. The sharks use these to attach the egg cases to rocks, seaweed, plant-like animals, such as sea whips, and other fixed items.

### BABIES ALIVE!

Hammerheads and some requiem sharks have live young with placentas and umbilical cords. Placental sharks may have only a few pups or as many as a hundred. Most sharks have two uteri, unlike mammals, which have only one.

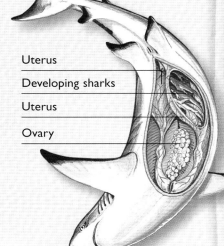

Uterus

Developing sharks

Uterus

Ovary

Female grey reef shark

### WEDGING EGGS IN CREVICES

Horn sharks lay oval egg cases ringed with a spiral of ridges like a screw. The mother wedges the egg cases into cracks and crevices, where the ridges hold them firmly and safely. Each species of horn shark lays a slightly different shape of egg case.

*Juvenile zebra shark*    *Adult zebra shark*

# Shark Meets World

CAN A SHARK be called a teenager? It may sound strange, but it's not far off the mark. Like all animals – including humans – sharks take time to grow and mature. They even go through a period like human adolescence, where they undergo rapid physical changes that leave them ready to breed. For the males, it means that the claspers grow. For the females, it means that their ovaries begin to develop eggs. At this point, sharks are sexually mature, or ready to have babies.

How long a shark takes to become a breeding adult varies with each species. Smaller species, such as bonnetheads and leopard sharks, mature quickly. Larger ones, such as dusky sharks and great whites, can take longer.

Sharks go through other physical changes before they reach 'adolescence' too. As well as growing larger, some species, such as zebra sharks, change their colour or skin patterns. Others, such as great whites and horn sharks, eat different foods as they mature, so their teeth change shape to cope with the difference.

**FASTEST-GROWING SHARK**
Shark species that are small at birth tend to grow faster than larger sharks. This smallish (1 metre/3 ft) sharpnose shark has a lifespan of 10 or 15 years but may reach maturity within a year of its birth.

A 10-year-old dusky shark is about 1.5 metres (5 ft) long.

A one-year-old dusky shark measures just less than 1.2 metres (4 ft).

**TEN YEARS STRONG**
A 10-year-old human girl averages 1.4 metres (4 ft 8 in) in height. She is some years away from sexual maturity and is still dependent on her parents. Sexual maturity for a dusky shark of the same age is also some years away.

**STARTING OUT**
At birth, most human babies weigh about 2.5–5 kilograms (5–10 lbs) and are between 48–58 centimetres (19–23 in) long. A newborn dusky shark is almost 1 metre (3 ft) long. A baby dusky shark has to fend for itself, but the human baby is completely dependent on its parents for survival.

**IN THE BEGINNING**
Just after a shark egg is laid, the yolk is large and clearly visible. But you would need a magnifying glass to see the tiny shark embryo as it rests on top of the yolk.

The young shark gets food from the yolk through a tube connected to its intestine.

**WHAT'S INSIDE...**
One swellshark egg case holds one growing shark and a fat-filled yolk that feeds it. Laid in cold water, a shark's egg may take a year to hatch. Young sharks develop more quickly in warmer water.

Eggs are laid in amber-coloured cases known as mermaids' purses.

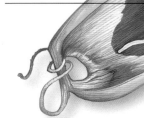

## Word Builders

- **Adolescence** is based on two Latin words – *ad-*, a prefix for 'toward', and *alescere*, which means 'to grow' or 'to be nourished'.
- Something that grows within – like a baby – is an **embryo**. It comes from the Greek *enbryein*, meaning 'to swell'.

## That's Amazing!

- How do scientists tell the age of a dead shark? Much the same way that botanists count the rings in a tree trunk. Marine scientists stain a shark's vertebrae – the bones of the spinal column – then count the rings in one or more of the largest vertebrae. Most sharks produce one new ring each year.
- Most kinds of sharks live to be about 25 years old, but spiny dogfish have been known to live for 100 years.

## Pathfinder

- How do shark young hide in plain sight? Go to page 22.
- Learn how baby sharks are made on pages 38–39.
- Sometimes newborn sharks become shark food. What's a mother to do? Find out on pages 42–43.

At age 20, the dusky shark is about 2.3 metres (7.5 ft) long. It won't stop growing completely until it dies, at about 40 years of age and a length of about 3 metres (10 ft).

### TWENTY YEARS AND MORE

By age 20, humans can survive on their own and have reached their full height – about 2 metres (6 ft) in males. Most wait until their 20s to start a family, although they've been sexually mature for years. Dusky sharks, in contrast, are just reaching sexual maturity at this age.

### INSIDE STORY

## In the Nursery

Dr Samuel Gruber, who runs a summer course to teach young people about sharks, has been studying lemon sharks around Bimini Island in the Bahamas for 30 years. By tagging them, he and his students have learnt how fast they grow. 'At first we thought lemon sharks grew fast, maturing in two to three years. Now we know that they grow very slowly indeed. After four years in the nursery shallows, they have grown only about 40 centimetres (16 in). And they may not mature for 15–20 years.' Adult lemon sharks can grow to 3.4 metres (11 ft) in length.

### NEARLY THERE

As the young shark absorbs the yolk and develops, it gets larger and the yolk gets smaller. The baby shark breathes through well-developed gills.

The newborn shark pup emerges from the splitting egg case.

### HATCHING

When the young shark, or pup, has completely absorbed the yolk and developed into a miniature adult, it hatches from its flexible egg case. The shark is on its own. It must be especially careful not to become food for larger creatures like groupers and adult sharks.

*Newborn tiger shark*                    *Newborn zebra shark*

# The Game of Life

LIFE IN THE OCEAN is a continuous and dangerous game of hide-and-seek. The simple truth is that sharks eat everything – including other sharks. But many have developed ways to improve their chances of survival in order to pass their genes to the next generation.

Take tiger sharks, who produce a large number of small young. The bigger the numbers, the greater the chances are that some will survive. The downside is that these defenceless young are likely to become fish food. Great whites take a different kind of gamble. Mother whites produce only a few young, but the young are relatively large. This is an advantage, but the lack of numbers is a risk.

Shark mothers provide no care for either live pups or eggs. Instead, they concentrate on finding the safest birthing environment for their young. Live bearers will choose shallow bays free of large predators as nurseries. Egg-layers hide their eggs in crevices or seaweed.

Many newborn sharks, such as zebras and whiskery sharks, have protective markings or coloration that keeps them out of sight. Some, such as baby whitetip reef sharks, are preyed on by the adults of the species, so the babies hide among the corals, safely out of reach. Even adult whitetips are at risk of being eaten by larger sharks. So they've learnt to hide in caves by day, coming out to hunt at night under cover of darkness.

**PRICKLY PREY**
A horn shark's colour and pattern help it to blend into the background. If a predator should spot it, this shark also has two sharp spines on its back to help it survive the encounter. It can wedge itself in a rocky crevice with its back and spines pointing outwards. Few predators will risk trying to eat that prickly mouthful.

**SWELL IDEA**
A swellshark resists attack by first wedging itself in a crack and then inflating its stomach with water until it is firmly stuck. Predators find it impossible to pull the balloon-like shark from its hiding place.

## INSIDE STORY

### A Flash of Terror

American Mike de Gruy is a marine biologist and professional film-maker. His work has taken him to many places, and one he won't forget in a hurry is Enewetak Atoll in the South Pacific. 'I was using my flash camera to take photos of grey reef sharks. I needed a flash because the white bellies of grey reefs blend with the light from above, and you can't see their darker tones. If you're beneath them, looking up, they are almost invisible. I got some good "looking-up" shots. Then I noticed one smaller shark starting the typical threat posture. "What a shot!" I thought. I tripped my flash and – bang! The shark grabbed my arm and shook it. I dropped the camera, losing my amazing pictures forever. I made it back to the boat, bleeding from my wound. No pictures, but I've got a great scar to remind me of that two-tone shark!'

*Newborn grey carpetshark and its egg case*

*Newborn whiskery shark and its yolk sac*

## Word Builders

• Animals display **agonistic** behaviour when they confront possible aggressors or competitors. The word comes from the Latin *agonista*, meaning 'competitor'.
• A **generation** is a group of beings born and living at roughly the same time. The word comes from the Latin *genus*, meaning 'descent' or 'birth'.

## That's Amazing!

• To scare off predators, sand tiger sharks will swim straight at them, then turn away suddenly so that their tail hits the water with an ear-splitting crack – a behaviour called tail-cracking.
• For some sharks, the fight for survival starts in the womb. In some species, including pelagic threshers and sand tigers, the first embryo to hatch inside each uterine chamber survives by eating the others.

## Pathfinder

• How often do some sharks need to eat to survive? Find the answer on pages 16–17.
• How do sharks disguise themselves to hide from predators? Read more about it on pages 22–23.
• Deep-sea fish have developed special adaptations to survive in an inhospitable world. See pages 56–57.

Galápagos shark

## LOOK OUT!

A wolf bares its teeth, arches its back and lowers its head to warn off an aggressor. This is called agonistic behaviour. A grey reef shark also uses threatening postures to scare off an enemy, such as a diver. It points its pectoral fins down, arches its back and moves its head from side to side. The more agitated the shark becomes, the more intense the display. A sensible aggressor will immediately back off at such a sight.

Agonistic side view

Agonistic front view

Agonistic top view

## A CROWDED HOUSE

Many sharks must always keep moving forwards in order to breathe. Others, such as these whitetip reef sharks, can rest for periods of time during the day. They breathe by pumping water containing oxygen over their gills. To rest in safety, they must find shelter from predators. There is not much hiding space among the coral reefs for creatures this size, so many whitetips crowd together to share a cave.

*Grouper – a danger
to young sharks*

*Killer whale – a
shark predator*

# Shark Food

IF IT SWIMS in the sea and it's bigger than the nail on your little finger, it is probably suitable food for a shark. Of course, the shark has to track down this prey, and different prey animals have various methods to escape capture. As predators at the top of the food chain, sharks are good at tracking prey – using their keen senses. Individual species may also have particular hunting styles, depending on their food choices.

Some sharks, such as the mako and great white, simply outswim their prey. Others hunt in groups, allowing them to tackle even very large schools of food fishes. The filter-feeders generally swim around with mouths agape, scooping up their food. Still other sharks use camouflage to take prey by surprise.

Even though sharks are hunters, they are sometimes the hunted as well. Young and small sharks of many species are eaten by other, larger fish, such as groupers or adult sharks, and even toothed whales.

## WATCH THE BIRDY

Seabirds nest in big colonies on many low, sandy, tropical islands. Young birds, like this albatross fledgling, take off from land and can crash into nearby shallows when they are just learning to fly. If they are lucky, the wind and their paddling feet return them to the beach for another try. If they are unlucky, a cruising tiger shark rushes up from beneath, snatches them and gulps them down.

## SCHOOL'S OUT

Some fish swim in large schools because there is usually safety in numbers. But this is not true when the predator is a blue shark. Normally unable to catch anything from a swirling mass of schooling fish, the blue sharks shown here are breaking up the mass into smaller groups. Some fish will lose their place and become easy prey.

Reef sharks swallow fish like this harlequin tuskfish whole.

Cephalopods, such as squid, are a favourite food of blue sharks and some kinds of hammerhead.

The hard shells of lobsters and crabs don't protect them from the powerful jaws and teeth of hungry sharks.

## WHAT'S ON THE MENU?

Sharks used to be thought of as the dustbins of the sea, eating whatever they could find. While tiger sharks have been known to eat just about anything – including kangaroos and cows that have washed down flooded rivers, as well as plastic bags and cans of food – other species are more discerning. Most species of shark eat a variety of animals, allowing them to find enough to eat, even if one type of prey is in short supply. Others have very specialized diets. The California horn shark, for example, feeds on sea urchins.

## Word Builders

• A **predator** is an animal that eats other animals. The word comes from the Latin *praeda* – the same word that gives us the word 'prey'.
• A **frenzy** is a state of agitation or excitement. The word comes from the Latin *phrensis*, meaning 'mind'.

## That's Amazing!

• What do California sea otters and horn sharks have in common? Pink skeletons! Both feed on purple sea urchins. Pigment from the sea urchins enters the bloodstream. It then combines with calcium in the growing cartilage of sharks or skeletons of sea otters, tinting them pink.
• Some sluggish bottom-dwellers, such as swellsharks, have survived for more than a year in captivity without eating.

## Pathfinder

• Some sharks really use their heads when they hunt for food. Find out about them on pages 18–19.
• Do sharks have special cutlery for special food? Read up on teeth and jaws on pages 36–37.
• What's on the menu for developing shark embryos? Turn to pages 40–41.

### STIR CRAZY

The 'feeding frenzies' seen in films have usually been provoked by people throwing bloody bait into the water. Sharks seldom behave in this way in the wild. Scavenging tiger sharks, for example, will appear completely calm around a dead whale and tend to avoid one another, even while feeding.

### INSIDE STORY

## Bite and Spit

Peter Pyle is a biologist with the Point Reyes Bird Observatory in California, U.S.A. On the Farallon Islands, west of San Francisco, he has observed the attack and feeding behaviour of great white sharks. 'From the high cliffs I would see a shark approaching a seal,' he reports. 'The shark charged, took a bite and then backed off while the seal died. This is called 'bite and spit' feeding.' This feeding method does two things. It lets the shark taste the prey to see if it will make a good meal. It also conserves energy, because blood loss, rather than hard work on the part of the shark, will eventually kill the prey.

Rays are some of the largest fish in the sea, but that doesn't stop sharks from attacking and eating them.

A tiger shark can munch through a sea turtle's hard shell.

Seals are a favourite food of great whites.

Cookiecutter sharks take biscuit-shaped chunks out of dolphins and other large prey.

# A Shark's World

NOW THAT YOU'VE learnt something about sharks – inside and out – it's time to see them in action. First, we'll look at creatures that have managed to find a way to live with these ocean predators. Then, after a visit to a reef and some cool-water shallows, we'll head out to the open ocean. From there we'll descend through the murky mid-waters and into the deepest, darkest layer of the sea. Sharks share their watery world with some of the most fantastic creatures, and you're about to meet them face to face. So get ready to dive right in...

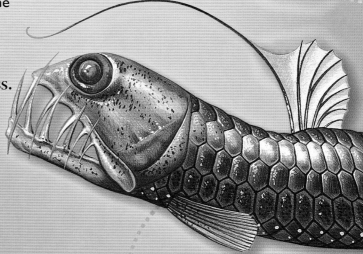

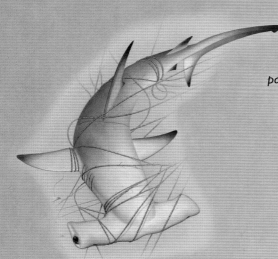

# Hangers-On

WHILE MOST SHARKS are loners, they never really swim alone. Sharks carry a variety of marine passengers, both inside and outside their bodies. First, there are parasites. Many kinds of worm live inside a shark's intestinal tract, while leeches and crab-like copepods live on a shark's outside – leeches near the mouth and cloaca, and copepods near gill slits, fins and even on the eyes. Parasites such as these actually feed on their host, in this case a shark, but they don't usually weaken it to the point of death. They must strike a delicate balance so that their host will continue to provide them with food.

Other companions are not nearly so harmful. Pilot fish and remoras are a shark's most frequent attendants. Pilot fish ride pressure waves in front of the shark, and remoras attach themselves to the shark itself with suction. Pilot fish are opportunists who take advantage of the shark's feeding habits to live off the leftovers. Remoras have a symbiotic relationship with sharks, which means that both parties benefit – the remoras make a good living eating the parasites that live off the sharks, and the sharks get a free cleaning service.

## PAYING THEIR WAY
Remoras, which can attach and detach at will, can be found on the underside or back of their hosts. The eight different species have distinct preferences. Some are found with rays and sharks, such as this Caribbean reef shark, and others with whales or sea turtles. But providing sharks with a cleaning service doesn't always guarantee the remoras' safety.

Sandbar shark

Remora

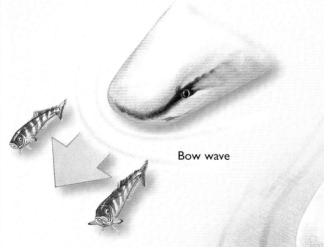

Bow wave

## UNDERWATER SURFING
When a streamlined object moves through water, it creates pressure waves in front of it. The waves created in front of a shark help to push along smaller swimmers.

## HELPING HANDS
King angelfish usually eat sponges, sea squirts and other animals attached to the rocky bottom. But when a shark swims by, the angelfish swim up to dine on parasites that live on it. Sharks accept the services of these and many other 'cleaners' and stay still as the visitors groom and clean them.

## FREE MEALS?
Pilot fish get protection from their travelling companions the sharks because not many predators will risk hunting near a shark. The smaller fish manage to get some good meals out of the scraps the sharks leave. But they have to watch their backs, or they can become shark food themselves.

Pilot fish

King angelfish

## Word Builders

- A **parasite** is an animal that lives by taking substances, such as blood, from other animals. Although parasites don't usually kill their hosts, they don't help them either. The word comes from the Greek for 'one who lives at another's expense'.
- **Remora** is from the Latin for 'delay'. These fish, which also attach themselves in large numbers to boats, were once thought to slow ships down.

## That's Amazing!

- Some kinds of parasitic worm will live in only one species of shark. When the first megamouth shark was discovered, its stomach contained a new species of worm that has never been found in any other kind of shark.
- Do parasites affect shark behaviour? Maybe. Makos have been known to leap from the water. Scientists think they do it to shake off irritating parasites.

## Pathfinder

- Sharks like some shrimps for their grooming service and others for their food value. Learn more on pages 16–17.
- Pilot fish use hydrodynamics to surf the bow waves in front of sharks. See how hammerheads employ hydrodynamics on pages 18–19.
- Cleaner fish that are swallowed by sharks sometimes find an ingenious escape route. See page 33.

## PERSONAL GROOMING

Copepods, often known as sea lice, are small crustaceans that feed on the skin tissue of their hosts. They usually attach themselves to fins or gills, but one species latches onto the corneas of Greenland sharks' eyes, as shown here.

## REEF CARETAKERS

Several kinds of coral reef and kelp bed animals make their living by cleaning larger animals, such as sharks. Sharks visit these 'cleaning stations' just as you might go to a dentist. Some cleaners even swim into the shark's mouth looking for parasites to eat.

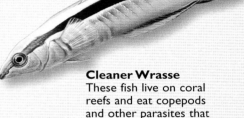

**Cleaner Wrasse**
These fish live on coral reefs and eat copepods and other parasites that live on sharks.

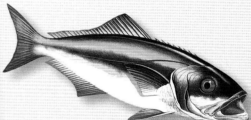

**Cobias**
Fish called cobias, relatives of the remora, hang around larger fish, including sharks, for protection. They also keep the reef clean by eating scraps from the other fishes' meals.

## HANDS ON

### All-day Sucker

How does a remora manage to hold on to a shark? The answer is suction. That's what allows a cup-shaped object to stick to a smooth surface after the air is removed. This is called a vacuum. Remoras make a vacuum with ridges of special muscles, which are actually modified dorsal fins, on top of their heads.

You can try this for yourself. Take a rubber suction cup like the plunger shown here, press it onto a smooth surface such as a refrigerator door, and press out the air. Now pull. The plunger sticks to the door because the weight of the Earth's atmosphere is pressing down on it. In the case of the remora, the weight of the surrounding water presses against it to hold it in place.

**Banded Coral Shrimp**
Sharks will remain very still while the cleaner shrimp does its job along the gills and in the shark's mouth.

# Riot on the Reef

CORAL POLYPS ARE the architects of the sea. These tiny creatures can transform an underwater desert, containing no nutrients or inhabitants, into a thriving colony where other plant and animal life abounds.

A new reef is formed when free-floating coral larvae are carried on ocean currents away from their reef of origin. Once they reach shallow water, they take up residence. First they attach themselves to hard surfaces. Then they use a symbiotic algae that lives in their gut to convert chemicals in sea water into stony, exterior skeletons. The skeletons make huge underwater structures – the coral reefs. These reefs provide food and shelter for a riot of plant and animal life, such as seaweed, algae, shellfish, sponges, sea urchins, starfish and fish – including sharks.

Indo-Pacific reefs are home to blacktip reef sharks, whitetip reefs, grey reefs, tiger and Galápagos sharks. Caribbean reefs support Caribbean reef sharks, lemon, bull, sandbar and tiger sharks. These many types of shark have developed different feeding habits and tastes to avoid competing with each other for food.

Jellyfish are related to corals and sea anemones.

The grey reef shark is a top predator of the coral reef.

Octopus hide in the reef and hunt crabs.

Grey reef shark

## INSIDE STORY

### The Living Coral

Dr Bruce Carlson is a marine biologist who studies corals and coral reefs. He also directs the Waikiki Aquarium in Hawaii where corals are displayed and reared. 'Spawning corals are a magical sight! I saw them once on a dive in the Pacific off the Solomon Islands. It was during a full moon in November — species always spawn at the same time every year — and the corals released millions of eggs and clouds of sperm into the water at once. The amazing part is that we were able to predict the exact night of the spawning.'

## FOOD CHAIN GANG

Tiny fish get eaten by small fish, and the small fish get eaten by larger ones. But sometimes the chain of events gets more complicated. In this reef food chain, damselfish feed snappers, which feed jacks, which feed grey reef sharks. But what feeds the damselfish? The eggs of the jack. This complex food chain is called a food web.

## Word Builders

- **Polyps** have many tentacles. They get their name from the Latin *polypus*, for 'many-footed'.
- The eight-legged **octopus** is named for its shape. *Okto* is Greek for 'eight', and *pous* is Greek for 'foot'.
- **Spawn** is both a verb – to deposit eggs – and a noun – the mass of eggs themselves. It comes from the Old French *spandre*, meaning 'to spread out or expand'.

## That's Amazing!

- Australia's Great Barrier Reef is 2,012 kilometres (1,250 mi) long – the largest coral reef in the world, and the only natural structure that is visible from outer space. It can be seen clearly from the Moon, 384,000 km (239,000 mi) above the Earth.
- Sponges are extremely efficient filter-feeders. They can process 1,000 times their own bulk of water per hour.

## Pathfinder

- Which shark relatives find their food in the sand? The answer is on pages 24–25.
- Coral and algae are symbionts. Do sharks have symbiotic relationships? See pages 48–49.
- Should you swim with a Caribbean reef shark? Only if you're careful! Find out more on pages 60–61.

## LIFE IN THE CORAL

Tiny coral polyps, each no bigger than a pinhead, can team up to become mighty builders. Other creatures benefit from the stony homes built by coral polyps. Thousands of kinds of animals all find places to hunt and hide. Marine plants grow on the coral structures and provide food for many reef creatures.

Cleaner wrasse pick parasites off bigger fish.

## KEEPING WARM

In the warmer months of the year, crowds of pregnant grey reef sharks come into shallow water and mill around. Marine scientists think that the warmer water helps the shark foetuses to develop at a faster rate inside their mothers.

Parrotfish

Yellow tang

Clownfish find protection from predators by living among the stinging tentacles of sea anemones, and they don't get stung themselves.

Colourful reef fish like this double-saddled butterflyfish use their markings to hide themselves among the brightly coloured corals.

Sponges attach themselves to the reef and feed on tiny particles, including coral polyp eggs, that they filter from the water.

Damselfish

Jack

Snapper

Jack eggs

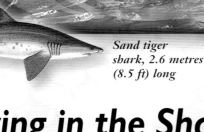

*Sand tiger shark, 2.6 metres (8.5 ft) long*

*Bonnethead shark, 1 metre (3 ft) long*

*Sandbar shark, 2 metres (6.5 ft) long*

# Living in the Shallows

SUNLIGHT HELPS shallow coastal waters to be areas of high biodiversity – places where many kinds of organisms live. Marine plants of all types use sunlight to make food. But plants need nutrients to grow best. The richest plant growth thrives along coastlines, where natural substances, such as silt, wash from the land to nourish the plants. Many different kinds of animals live in these shallows, feeding off these plants – or off one another. A swim through the turtle-grass beds growing in the warm waters off the coast of Florida in the U.S.A., or the kelp forests of a cool California sea, reveals an amazing richness of life. And, as usual, sharks are at the top of the connected food chains.

Swimmers in the cool waters of the Pacific Ocean kelp beds may see the most dangerous shark of all – the great white. But it's far more likely that they will see smaller, harmless sharks, such as horn sharks, leopard sharks, swellsharks and angel sharks.

The warm shallows of the Atlantic Ocean are home to a greater number of larger sharks – bull sharks, tiger sharks, sandbar sharks, lemon sharks and Caribbean reef sharks. Here they can feed on fish such as menhaden and herrings, and even sea turtles.

**SHALLOWS VERSUS REEF**
The habitats known as shallows are those along continental coasts. Nutrient-rich waters such as these are usually green and sometimes murky, like the waters off California, U.S.A. Coral reefs often form in shallow water, but corals need clear water in which to get established, and the clearest waters are far from coastlines. Coral reefs are therefore not the same as areas known as shallows. Shallows can be found in all the world's temperature zones.

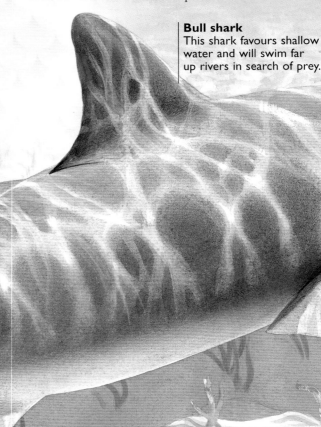

**Bull shark**
This shark favours shallow water and will swim far up rivers in search of prey.

**Nudibranchs**
Colourful sea slugs, called nudibranchs, live in the zone between high and low tide. They feed on invertebrates. When they meet others of their species, they often fight, biting and eating chunks of each other.

**Purple shore crab**
This crab eats mainly algae, but also scavenges dead animals.

## COOL CUSTOMERS

The sheltered rocks at the bottom of a cool-water kelp forest are home to many creatures, both mobile and sedentary. All have relatives in the warm shallows of turtle-grass beds and on coral reefs. Mobile animals, such as crabs, nudibranchs and starfish, move around and hunt for food. Sedentary animals, such as sea anemones, sea squirts and sponges, can't move. They are attached to surfaces and must wait for ocean currents to bring food, in the form of plankton, to them. To protect themselves, many of these animals have spines or armour. Others can sting or inject their enemies with poison.

## Word Builders

- **Biodiversity** is a new word formed from *bios*, Greek for 'life', and diversity, from Latin *divergere*, 'to turn aside' or 'to take different paths'.
- **Spine** has two meanings – a sharp-tipped spike, and the backbone of an animal. It comes from the Latin *spina*, meaning both 'thorn' and 'backbone'.
- **Nudibranchs** are so called because of their external gills. Their name is a combination of the Latin words *nudus*, 'naked', and *branchia*, 'gills'.

## That's Amazing!

- Some sharks can poison people. The meat of whitetip reef sharks can cause ciguatera, a type of food poisoning that involves severe stomach cramps.
- Some nudibranchs 'borrow' the stinging tentacles of the sea anemones that they feed on. Somehow, these tentacles are not digested by the nudibranch, but become part of the animal's own appendages. And they work, too. When a predator attacks a nudibranch, it gets a stinging mouthful.

## Pathfinder

- Horn sharks lay unusual eggs. Read about them on pages 38–39.
- The sea's largest structures are built by some of its smallest animals. Find out more on pages 50–51.
- Not all shallows are frequented by sharks, but it's useful to know how to avoid a shark attack just in case. Turn to pages 60–61.

A sea turtle in the shallows may be unaware of a bull shark approaching.

Jacks

**A SHARK WITH HORNS**

The California horn shark is one of nine living species of horn shark. These sharks usually grow to 60 centimetres (2 ft) long, but can reach twice that size. A large spine in front of each dorsal fin gives them their name. They live in cool water among large rocks at the base of kelp beds. Their strange, screw-like egg cases and distinctive looks make them popular exhibits in public aquariums. Fossil records show that this family of sharks has remained virtually unchanged for 160 million years.

**DANGER IN THE SHALLOWS**

Shallow waters, like the warm waters of the Florida turtle-grass beds pictured here, are rich with food. But for a shark's prey, eating can be dangerous. If an animal, such as a turtle, lets down its guard for a minute, it runs the risk of being gobbled up as it feeds. When shallow waters are clear, it makes hunting easy for sharks, because they usually have good vision. However, their prey can also see them sooner than in murky water and have more chance of avoiding being a shark's meal.

## HANDS ON

# Getting in Touch

Most aquariums have 'touch-tanks' where you can learn what some sea creatures, such as small sharks and rays, starfish and sea urchins, feel like. You can touch the denticles on sharks, the spines of sea urchins and the skeletons of coral. Some animals have surprising textures. For example, some starfish look soft, but are actually rock hard. And the egg cases of horn sharks feel so much like flexible plastic that most people can't believe they're real.

**Sea anemones**
These animals have stinging tentacles. Some anemones reproduce by splitting themselves in pieces. Each piece forms a new individual.

**Starfish**
Known to eat shellfish and coral polyps, starfish push their stomachs out of their mouths to surround prey. Once digested, the food is then sucked up into the starfish's digestive glands.

**Sea squirts**
These animals attach themselves to rocks and are sometimes mistaken for plants. A large sea squirt can pump 18–22 litres (4–5 gal) of sea water a day to filter its food, obtain oxygen and pass waste products.

*Crocodile shark, 90 centimetres (3 ft) long*

*Prickly dogfish, 75 centimetres (2.5 ft) long*

*Necklace carpetshark, 90 centimetres (3 ft) long*

# Making It in the Mid-waters

THE OPEN OCEAN is a vast expanse of water. To make it easier to study, scientists have divided it into layers. The first layer is the one we can see – the upper waters near the surface. The bottom of the deep sea, or the abyss, is another layer. But the biggest layer by far is the mid-waters – 300 metres (1,000 ft) below the surface yet far above the abyss, which can be 10,900 metres (35,425 ft) deep. The further down you go, the darker it is. Sea water is so dense that it filters out the sunlight. And this is the key to life in the mid-water layer. Somehow the animals that live there have learned to cope with little or no sunlight.

Tiny plants called phytoplankton form the basis of the ocean's food chain. To make food, they need light so they live near the surface of the water. Tiny animals, or zooplankton, feed on these plants, as do fish and other sea creatures. Since there's plenty of food in this upper layer, some mid-water sharks, such as cookiecutters and megamouths, migrate upwards to feed. Others, such as catsharks and sleeper sharks, stay put and dine on their deep-living neighbours.

## STRUGGLE IN THE DEPTHS
In the life-or-death struggle to survive in the mid-waters layer, the small animals get eaten by the large ones, and the sharks usually eat them all. Pictured below is a confrontation between two large mid-water predators – a frill shark and a giant squid. Because they live hidden in the deep, we know very little about either species. In fact, no-one has ever seen a living giant squid and it is quite possible that the shark is the prey and the squid is the predator. The deep mid-waters hide many large creatures and some may still remain undiscovered. Others, such as the megamouth shark, are hardly known.

## PRIMITIVE SPECIMEN
The ruffled edges of its large gill slits give the frill shark its name. Frill sharks grow to 2 metres (6.5 ft) long and feed on squid, fish and other sharks. These sharks resemble fossilized sharks that lived on Earth 200 million years ago.

## HIDDEN PREDATOR
Named because of the way it takes bite-size chunks out of its prey, the cookiecutter shark stays hidden in deep mid-waters below 600 metres (2,000 ft) by day. At night, it swims up to the surface to stalk swordfish, tuna, dolphins, other sharks and even large whales.

*Bramble shark, 2.2 metres (7.25 feet) long*

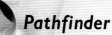

## Word Builders

Names for the layers of the sea come from Greek words. **Pelagios** means 'open sea', **epi** means 'upper', **meso** means 'middle', and **abyss** means 'deeper than you can imagine'. **Epipelagic** is surface to 300 metres (1,000 ft) deep, **mesopelagic** is 300–1,500 metres (1,000–5,000 ft) deep and **abysso-pelagic** is more than 1,500 metres (5,000 ft) down.

## That's Amazing!

• Cookiecutter sharks don't just attack other fish. One has even been known to take a bite out of the rubber dome of a nuclear submarine.
• Large eyes absorb more light – useful in deep, dark waters. A giant squid's eye is 40 centimetres (16 in) across – the size of a large pizza.

## Pathfinder

• To learn more about sharks that feed exclusively on plankton, see pages 16–17.
• Do sharks need to see to find food? Find out on pages 30–31.
• Do sharks live in the deepest waters of all? Go to page 56.

### TENTACLED TERROR
Giant squid are the largest invertebrates in the world. With tentacles outstretched, they can be as long as 18 metres (60 ft). A squid might release a large ink cloud to confuse predators or prey.

## IN DEEP MID-WATERS

Sharks are not the only creatures in the deep middle layers of the open sea. Many of the world's strangest fish live there, too. Prey is scarce and hard to find in the dark, and so are mates, so deep-sea dwellers need special features to help them to survive and breed.

**Bristlemouth**
Light organs on their bellies help them to see prey and to find potential mates.

**Dragonfish**
A movable, glowing lure on the chin attracts prey and is thought to help these fish signal to others of their species.

### DEEP-SEA GOBLIN
The bizarre-looking, pinkish-grey goblin shark grows to 3.9 metres (12.75 ft) and is the only member of its family. It is rarely seen and little is known of it. Its long snout is packed with electro-sense organs that help it locate and catch prey.

**Lanternfish**
Tiny lights on their chests and bellies attract mates and provide camouflage through counter-shading in upper waters.

### INSIDE STORY
## The Wonder of Sharks

Gil van Dykhuizen loves his job at the Monterey Bay Aquarium in California, U.S.A. 'I go fishing for small mid-water sharks and then try to bring them back alive to display at the aquarium in our new deep-sea exhibit,' he says. For these sharks to survive in captivity, the darkness and extreme cold of their natural environment must be replicated. Because deep-living sharks are very sensitive to light, van Dykhuizen and other keepers are experimenting with different wavelengths of light, such as infrared, so that people can observe the sharks while they remain safely in the dark.

**Cross-toothed Perch**
This fish can open its mouth very wide, enabling it to swallow prey larger than itself.

*False catshark, 2.5 metres (8.25 ft) long*

# In Total Darkness

IN THE DARK depths of the ocean, more than 1,000 metres (3,000 ft) below the surface, lies a strange and mysterious world. At these depths, the water is freezing. It is pitch dark and the pressure is hundreds of times greater than it is at the surface. A variety of fish and other sea creatures have adapted to these conditions, and where there's a steady supply of fish for food, there are bound to be sharks.

Although humans cannot dive this deep, scientists can travel down in submarines or deep-water submersibles. Through the windows of these special vessels, they have already photographed the false catshark at 200–1,500 metres (700–5,000 ft), the tiny spined pygmy shark at 1,800 metres (6,000 ft), and the bluntnose sixgill at 2,000 metres (6,500 ft). We also know about some deep-sea sharks from people who fish with deep-sea drag nets. The Portuguese shark, caught at a depth of 3,660 metres (12,000 ft), was first identified in this way.

Some scientists have visited depths even greater than 3,660 metres (12,000 ft). There they found fish, including shark relatives like the skate and chimaera, but no sharks. Scientists are not sure why sharks do not live down here, but they think it's probably due to lack of food. Sharks have adapted to every other sea environment where they can find enough food.

## GLOW-IN-THE-DARK SHARK
No sunlight reaches the very deep sea, but many deep-sea animals produce their own light. They are described as bioluminescent. This spined pygmy shark's belly is covered with tiny organs that produce just enough light to equal the faint glow that filters down from the surface when it swims to upper waters to feed. This is called counter-shading and helps the shark to merge with the ocean so that it can't be seen by predators below.

Research subs use electric motors to move slowly along the seabed.

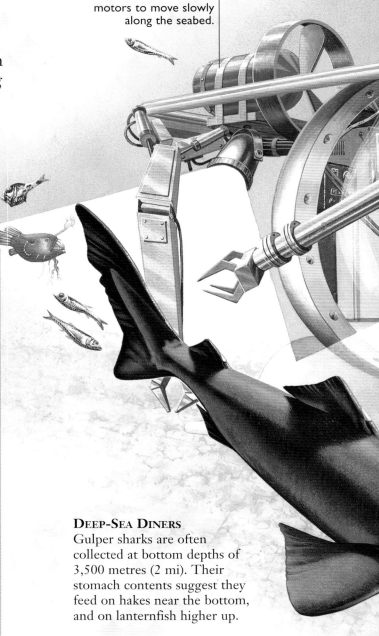

## INSIDE STORY
### A Trip Down Under

'Our sub, the *Pisces VI*, was just about to settle on the bottom, 600 metres (2,000 ft) deep off the island of Bermuda. I thought, "Gosh, I hope I can see something." Then, this huge, broad head came from underneath the sub, and the green eye of a shark was peering in as if looking at me.'

This is how scientist Eugenie Clark described an incident on one of more than 100 dives that she and deep-sea photographer Emory Kristof made in submersibles worldwide. These two Americans have added greatly to our knowledge of sharks. Kristof was a pioneer of direct deep-sea observation, and Clark catalogued the pair's discoveries. On a typical dive they took their vessel to the bottom and waited up to 17 hours for sharks and other creatures to come along.

## DEEP-SEA DINERS
Gulper sharks are often collected at bottom depths of 3,500 metres (2 mi). Their stomach contents suggest they feed on hakes near the bottom, and on lanternfish higher up.

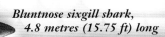

*Bluntnose sixgill shark, 4.8 metres (15.75 ft) long*

*Portuguese shark, 1 metre (3 ft) long*

## Word Builders

- **Bioluminescence** means light produced by a living animal, such as a firefly or a deep-sea fish. It comes from the Latin *bios*, meaning 'life', and *lumen*, meaning 'light'.
- **Bathyscaphe** is from the Greek word *bathys*, for 'deep', and *skaphe*, meaning 'a small boat or skiff'.

## That's Amazing!

The seabed in the deepest parts of the ocean is a virtual desert. No light ever reaches these depths, so there are no plants. Yet in some places, volcanic activity has created hot water vents. Here, a host of creatures, such as mussels, clams and huge tubeworms, thrive. What do they eat if there are no plants around? Bacteria. This was the first clue scientists had that not all food chains are plant-based.

## Pathfinder

- How does a shark see in the darkest waters? Go to pages 30–31.
- How deep are the layers of the ocean? Find out on pages 54–55.
- What could possibly threaten the deep sea's top predators? Learn more on pages 58–61.

## DEEP-SEA DENIZENS

Deep-sea fish have developed some strange adaptations to attract prey and escape from predators. These include special lures, large teeth, big mouths and stomachs that can expand to make the most of a rare meal, whatever the size. Some deep-sea fish have light organs on their bodies. These attract prey and also camouflage the fish when they migrate to upper levels of the sea to feed.

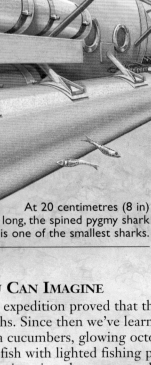

**SMALL BUT VALUABLE**
Little gulper sharks are caught off the coast of western Africa with deep-bottom trawls. A component in their oil-rich livers, and those of some other deep-water sharks, is used in cosmetics and medicinal drugs.

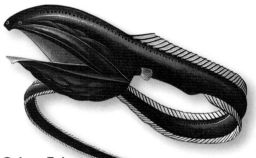

**Gulper Eel**
This eel's jaws are nearly one-quarter of its body length. A flashing pinkish light on its tail attracts prey.

**Hatchetfish**
Lights on their bellies camouflage these fish in the dimly lit mid-waters where they migrate each night to feed. Predators looking down see blackness. Those looking up see light – but no fish.

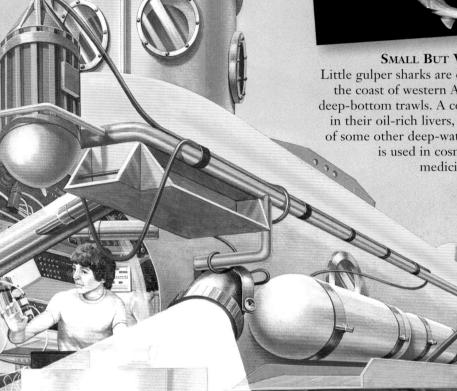

At 20 centimetres (8 in) long, the spined pygmy shark is one of the smallest sharks.

## DEEPER THAN YOU CAN IMAGINE

A late-19th century scientific expedition proved that the ocean is full of life at all depths. Since then we've learnt that creatures such as sponges, sea cucumbers, glowing octopus, shrimps that puff clouds and fish with lighted fishing poles live in very deep waters. Scientists view the ocean world from submersibles (once called bathyspheres and bathyscaphes). These vessels are made of steel and are designed to withstand tremendous water pressure. In 1960, the U.S. Navy bathyscaphe *Trieste* dived a record 10,910 metres (35,770 ft) – about 11 kilometres (7 mi) – into the Marianas Trench, the deepest known place on Earth.

**Viperfish**
When this fish eats prey with light organs, a special black stomach lining keeps the light from shining through the viperfish's flesh and exposing it to predators.

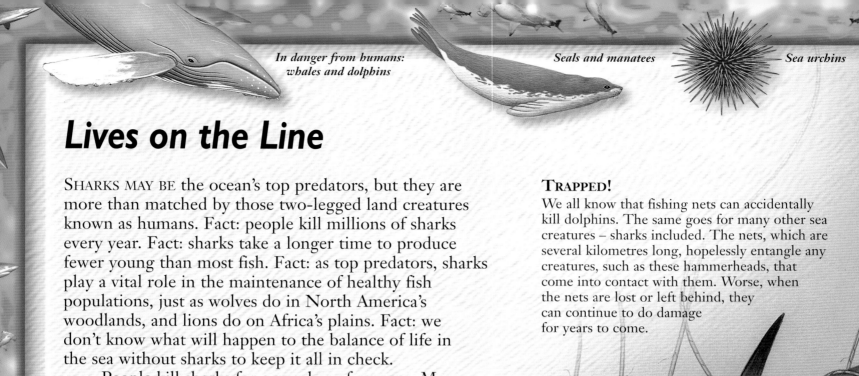

# Lives on the Line

SHARKS MAY BE the ocean's top predators, but they are more than matched by those two-legged land creatures known as humans. Fact: people kill millions of sharks every year. Fact: sharks take a longer time to produce fewer young than most fish. Fact: as top predators, sharks play a vital role in the maintenance of healthy fish populations, just as wolves do in North America's woodlands, and lions do on Africa's plains. Fact: we don't know what will happen to the balance of life in the sea without sharks to keep it all in check.

People kill sharks for a number of reasons. Many feel threatened by these large, mysterious predators and want to get rid of them for safety's sake. In Asia, an entire industry known as finning has emerged just to meet the huge demand for shark fins to make soup. People catch the shark, cut off its fins, then throw it back into the sea to drown or get eaten by other sharks. In addition, plenty of sharks die after becoming trapped in fishing nets. Some people let the sharks go, but many simply keep their catch. Such accidental captures are called bycatches.

Another threat to shark numbers is overfishing in general. Modern technology makes catching fish easier all the time. More fish are being caught and that cuts into the sharks' food supply.

Scalloped
hammerhead

## TRAPPED!

We all know that fishing nets can accidentally kill dolphins. The same goes for many other sea creatures – sharks included. The nets, which are several kilometres long, hopelessly entangle any creatures, such as these hammerheads, that come into contact with them. Worse, when the nets are lost or left behind, they can continue to do damage for years to come.

### CLEAN A BEACH – SAVE A SHARK

Have you ever walked along the beach and tripped over an empty tin or got your leg caught in a discarded fishing net? This kind of careless litter can destroy habitats and the creatures and plants that live in them. One way to help save all ocean animals is to join a volunteer beach clean-up crew like this one. A little effort goes a long way.

## Word Builders

- A **volunteer** is a person who willingly does something for the good of others without any payment or other reward. The word comes from the Latin *voluntas,* meaning 'will'.
- **Conservation** is the protection and careful management of the environment and natural resources such as plants and animals. It comes from the Latin *conservare,* 'to keep safe'.
- The Old English word for sheltered place – *haefen* – is the origin of **haven**.

## That's Amazing!

- More than 60,000 sharks were caught in Central and Western Pacific fisheries in 1998. Ninety-eight per cent of them were killed for their fins.
- For every single human killed by a shark, two million sharks are destroyed by humans. Twelve million sharks are killed by people each year, compared with six humans killed by sharks.

## Pathfinder

- What are the facts and figures about shark attacks on humans? Find out on pages 14–15.
- Just how many babies *can* a mother shark produce at one time? Go to pages 38–39.
- Can we live in harmony with dangerous predators such as sharks? Turn to pages 60–61 and read on.

Caribbean reef shark

### PARKS FOR SHARKS

Marine parks, such as Australia's Great Barrier Reef Park (above) and Ningaloo Reef Park, were set up to protect and observe life in reef waters. The parks balance conservation and tourism, and provide a safe haven for many types of shark. Divers from all over the world travel to these parks to swim with sharks like the gentle whale shark in their own environment.

INSIDE STORY

## Protecting Sharks

Dr Merry Camhi is working hard to stop careless finning and overfishing. She is the Senior Scientist of the National Audubon Society's Living Oceans Program. 'Our job is to convince the U.S. Congress and coastal state legislatures, as well as foreign governments, that sharks, rays and other large ocean fish are in real danger. We must work and act to save shark populations, and that means limiting catches to more reasonable levels.' The programme is also involved in protecting sharks' nursery grounds, as well as limiting recreational catches of sharks or, for some particularly vulnerable species, allowing only catch-and-release recreational fishing.

## TO DIE FOR

Some shark products are used to provide nutrients or medical products that improve human lives. Other shark products are luxuries. Many of these could be replaced with synthetic substitutes.

**Food**
Shark fins are an expensive delicacy, especially when the rest of the shark is thrown away. But some kinds of shark are sold for their meat as well as fins.

**Vitamins**
Oil obtained from a shark's liver is rich in vitamin A and other vital nutrients.

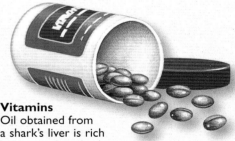

**Cosmetics**
Shark oil is also used in creams, lotions and lipsticks.

**Medical uses**
Shark corneas – the transparent covering of the eye – can be used to repair damaged human eyes.

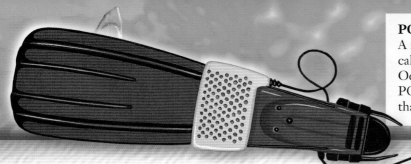

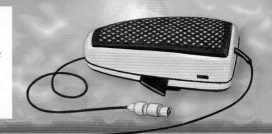

# Sharing the Water

SHARKS HAVE BEEN around for millions of years. They were swimming the world's oceans long before people arrived on the scene, and with luck, sharks will still be around millions of years from now – but only if we humans learn to play fair and share the water.

Although many people throughout history feared sharks, some people did not feel this way. In places such as Hawaii, Tahiti and Fiji, people lived close to the sea and knew their local sharks well. They realized that some sharks were dangerous, but that most were not. Some people even believed in the power of sharks to help and protect their human neighbours.

Today we are beginning to understand sharks better. As underwater technology improves, new species are being identified and more is being learned about the species we already know. Now that we know more about sharks, perhaps we can learn to treat them with the respect they deserve.

**TAKE CARE**
A confused shark is a dangerous shark, so never swim or dive in an area where a shark, such as this tiger shark, could mistake you for food or an enemy. Avoid rough or murky water and water that is polluted or has blood in it. Never swim alone.

Divers keep their arms folded so that they don't appear threatening to sharks.

**PLAYING TAG**
The best way to learn about sharks such as this lemon shark is to observe them in their habitat. But biologists also learn a lot by catching and tagging them and tracking them down later. Many things about sharks have been learnt in this way – including how fast they grow and how far they swim.

**KEEPING SHARKS AT BAY**
Generally, people feel more comfortable using protective gear around sharks. Chemicals, barriers and special suits are just a few of the ways – not all of them equally successful – in which humans try to stay safe in the water.

Life jacket with chemical repellent for shipwreck and air crash survivors at sea

U.S. Navy shark bag for survivors at sea

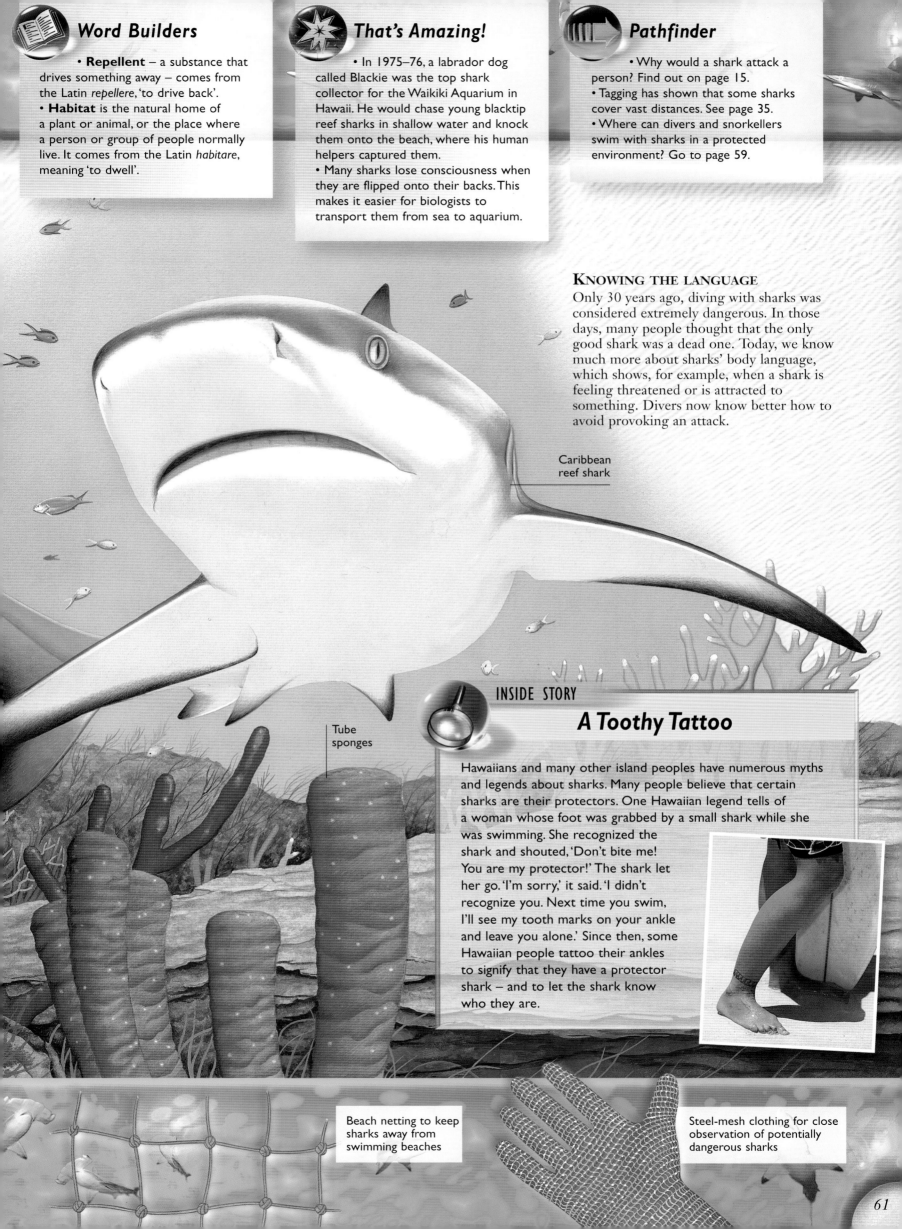

## Word Builders

• **Repellent** – a substance that drives something away – comes from the Latin *repellere*, 'to drive back'.
• **Habitat** is the natural home of a plant or animal, or the place where a person or group of people normally live. It comes from the Latin *habitare*, meaning 'to dwell'.

## That's Amazing!

• In 1975–76, a labrador dog called Blackie was the top shark collector for the Waikiki Aquarium in Hawaii. He would chase young blacktip reef sharks in shallow water and knock them onto the beach, where his human helpers captured them.
• Many sharks lose consciousness when they are flipped onto their backs. This makes it easier for biologists to transport them from sea to aquarium.

## Pathfinder

• Why would a shark attack a person? Find out on page 15.
• Tagging has shown that some sharks cover vast distances. See page 35.
• Where can divers and snorkellers swim with sharks in a protected environment? Go to page 59.

## KNOWING THE LANGUAGE

Only 30 years ago, diving with sharks was considered extremely dangerous. In those days, many people thought that the only good shark was a dead one. Today, we know much more about sharks' body language, which shows, for example, when a shark is feeling threatened or is attracted to something. Divers now know better how to avoid provoking an attack.

Caribbean reef shark

Tube sponges

### INSIDE STORY

# A Toothy Tattoo

Hawaiians and many other island peoples have numerous myths and legends about sharks. Many people believe that certain sharks are their protectors. One Hawaiian legend tells of a woman whose foot was grabbed by a small shark while she was swimming. She recognized the shark and shouted, 'Don't bite me! You are my protector!' The shark let her go. 'I'm sorry,' it said. 'I didn't recognize you. Next time you swim, I'll see my tooth marks on your ankle and leave you alone.' Since then, some Hawaiian people tattoo their ankles to signify that they have a protector shark – and to let the shark know who they are.

Beach netting to keep sharks away from swimming beaches

Steel-mesh clothing for close observation of potentially dangerous sharks

*Batoid*　　　　　　　*Caudal fin*　　　　　　　*Embryo*

# Glossary

**absorb** To soak up; a shark's intestines absorb the nutrients from its food.

**adaptation** A genetic characteristic of an animal that helps it to survive. Gills are an adaptation for breathing in water.

**anal** Relating to the area around an animal's anus. Most sharks have a single anal fin.

**aquarium** A container of fresh or salt water in which living plants and animals are kept. Also, a large institution, similar to a museum, where living ocean plants and animals are displayed and where scientists and students can study them.

**basking** Sun-bathing; lounging in sunlight.

**batoid** A member of the group of fish that includes all rays and skates.

**camouflage** A special colour or pattern on an animal's skin or fur that helps it blend into its surroundings, making it harder for predators or prey to see it.

**carnivorous** Meat-eating. Sharks, seals, cats, bears and dogs are all carnivorous animals.

**cartilage** A tough, flexible tissue that forms the skeleton in sharks and rays, and the outer ear and nose tip in humans.

**caudal** Relating to the area around an animal's tail. Caudal fin is another term for a fish's tail.

**cavity** A chamber within an animal that can contain some of the animal's organs.

**cloaca** A common opening for the digestive, excretory and reproductive tracts.

**cold-blooded** Having a body temperature matching that of the surrounding air or water. Most fish, including sharks, are cold-blooded.

**copepod** A tiny relative of shrimps and crabs that makes up most of the world's zooplankton. Some copepods are parasitic.

**courtship** The complex behaviour of two or more mature animals that leads to mating.

**denticle** A 'scale' on a shark's skin that is very similar to a tiny tooth.

**documentary** A factual film or television programme, such as a film about an historical event or the life and natural behaviour of a particular animal.

**dorsal** Relating to the area on an animal's back. Most sharks have two dorsal fins.

**electrical field** A space filled with electricity.

**embyro** An unborn animal or human in the first stages of development.

**enamel** A hard, glossy white coating that protects teeth.

**environment** All the physical and biological circumstances that surround an animal or group of animals.

**exterior** The outside of something.

**fertilization** The act of combining a sperm and egg to begin the development of a new individual.

**filament** A fine, thread-like fibre.

**filter-feeding** To eat by removing tiny food particles or creatures from a large volume of sea water. Whale sharks are filter-feeders.

**finning** The act of catching sharks, usually on a long-line, cutting off and selling their fins and discarding their bodies.

**foetus** An unborn animal or human in the later stages of development.

**food web** A complex inter-relationship of different species of animals that eat and are eaten by others.

**fossil** The ancient mineralized remains or traces of an animal or plant.

**gills** Special blood-filled structures that remove dissolved oxygen from water. Sharks, other fish, baby frogs and shellfish all use gills to breathe.

**habitat** The area in which a plant or animal lives.

**horizontal** In a side-to-side direction.

**hydrodynamics** The study of the way water moves.

**interior** The inside of something.

**invertebrate** An animal with no backbone. Sea urchins, starfish, shellfish and worms are all invertebrates.

**lateral line** A series of sensory organs along a shark's side that enables it to detect vibrations in the water.

**lobe** A protruding section of a larger organ or body part. Ears have lobes; so do livers. A shark's tail is divided into an upper lobe and a lower lobe.

**long-line** A way to catch large ocean animals by setting a line that is several kilometres long and that bears a series of baited hooks.

**lure** A decoy to attract an animal.

**microscopic** Something so small that it can be seen only with a microscope.

**mid-waters** A layer of the ocean that is some distance below the surface yet also far above the seabed.

*Food web*　　　　　　　*Hydrodynamics*

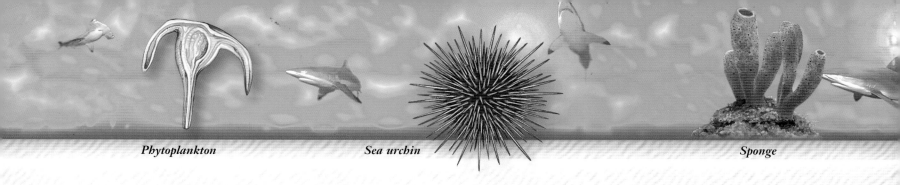

*Phytoplankton*

*Sea urchin*

*Sponge*

**migration** Seasonal movement of a group of animals from one place to another, often for breeding purposes or in search of food.

**muscle** Tissue made of elastic fibres that pull and relax to make a creature or human move.

**nerve** A bundle of energy-conducting fibres that connect the nervous system to muscles and organs.

**omnivorous** Eating a wide variety of plants and animals. Humans are omnivorous; sharks are carnivorous, or meat-eating.

**order** A category used by biologists who classify animals. An order contains families, which in turn contain genera and then species.

**organ** A complex of tissues that performs a specific function in an animal, such as the heart, brain or liver.

**organism** Any living thing, either plant or animal, of any size.

**oxygen** A chemical element vital for life. Its most common form is as a gas in air. Oxygen dissolves in water.

**parasite** An organism that benefits from the life of another creature and usually harms the creature in the process. Tapeworms, lice and fleas are all parasites.

**pectoral** Relating to the area around an animal's chest. All sharks have a pair of pectoral fins.

**pelagic** Relating to the wide open sea.

**pelvic** Relating to the area near the hips, or pelvis, or to the skeletal complex near the anus. Humans have a pelvic bone. Sharks have a pair of pelvic fins.

**phytoplankton** Tiny plants that form the basis of all ocean food chains.

**placenta** A spongy organ inside the uterus of a female human or animal that nourishes an embryo or foetus.

**plankton** Tiny plants and animals that drift with the ocean's currents.

**pollution** The contamination of air, water or land with harmful substances.

**predator** An animal – such as a mako shark, lion or wolf – that eats other living things and usually stalks or hunts them.

**pressure** A force that pushes on a certain area. The pressure in a liquid, such as water, acts in all directions.

**prey** Animals eaten by predators.

**propulsion** The process of driving or moving something in one direction.

**remora** A kind of fish that attaches itself to sharks and other large ocean creatures with suction via a modified dorsal fin.

**sea urchin** A round invertebrate animal, usually covered with stiff spines; a relative of starfish and sea cucumbers.

**seamount** An underwater mountain.

**serrated** Evenly and sharply notched along an edge. Many knives and some shark teeth have serrated edges.

**skeleton** The bony structure that supports an animal's body.

**species** All of the biologically similar animals that can mate with one another.

**spiracle** A small hole behind the eye of a shark or ray, sometimes used for breathing.

**sponge** A simple, aquatic, plant-like animal with a soft body wall.

**streamlined** Shaped to offer the least resistance to movement.

**submersible** An underwater vehicle used in ocean research; also called a research sub.

**symbiotic relationship** A situation in which plants and/or animals of different species live together in a way that benefits both parties.

**tissue** An organized mass of similar cells that work together.

**trawl** A large net that is dragged along the seabed, scraping up and catching everything that lives there.

**umbilical cord** A long flexible tube filled with blood vessels that connects a foetus to the placenta. This cord provides nourishment to a developing animal. Your navel, or belly button, marks the spot where the umbilical cord attached you to your mother's placenta when you were growing in her uterus.

**uterus** An organ inside a female animal's body in which a foetus develops. Also called the womb. Most sharks have two uteri. Mammals, including humans, have only one.

**vertebra** (plural **vertebrae**) One of a series of interlocking bones that make up the backbone.

**vertebrate** An animal with a backbone, such as an eagle, snake, shark, dolphin or dog.

**warm-blooded** Having a body temperature that is unaffected by the temperature of the surrounding air or water. Humans and mammals are all warm-blooded. Some sharks are also able to raise their body temperatures.

**wingspan** The straight distance from the tip of one wing to the tip of the other wing.

**zooplankton** Tiny animals that live in the ocean's surface layers.

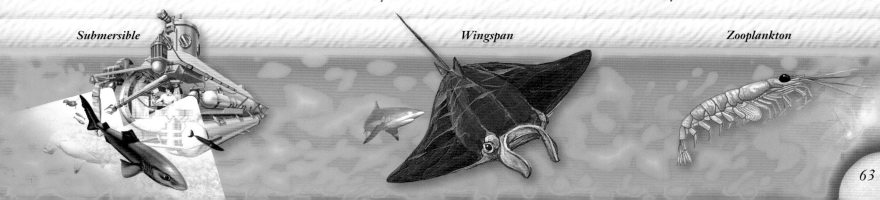

*Submersible*

*Wingspan*

*Zooplankton*

# Index

The publishers would like to thank the following people for their assistance in the preparation of this book: Barbara Bakowski, Dr. Lester Cannon, Katherine Gleason, Jill Goldowski, Dr. Craig Sowden. Our special thanks to the following children who feature in the photographs: Arianna Claridge, Julia Eger, William Eger, Frederick Marks, Christopher Stirling.

**PICTURE CREDITS** (t=top, b=bottom, l=left, r=right, c=center, e=extreme, f=flap, F=Front, C=Cover, B=Back). **Ad-Libitum** 5bc, 7c, 22cl, 29br, 40c, 41cl, 49bc (Mihal Kaniewski). **Aquarium of the Americas, New Orleans, LA** (Courtesy of John Hewitt) 33br. **Peter Arnold, Inc.** 37bl (Hanson Carroll). **Auscape International** 15dc (Doug Perrine), 50bl (Becca Saunders), 53tr (Mark Spencer). **Wayne and Karen Brown** 10t, 42tr. **Jan TenBruggencate** 36bc. **Merry Camhi** 59bc. **Bruce Coleman, Inc.** 19c (Norman Owen Tomalin), 34cl (Hans Reinhard), 14bl (Carl Roessler), 17t (Ron and Valerie Taylor). **Bob and Cathy Cranston** 23cr, 42cr (Bob Cranston). **Environmental Images** 59cr (Toby Adamson), 59c (Irene R. Lengui). **Al Giddings Images, Inc.** 37ct (Al Giddings). **Edward S. Hodgson** 30c. **Innerspace Visions** 30tl (Mark Conlin), 35br, 48tr (Bob Cranston), 51tr (Steve Drogin), 9tr (Richard Ellis), 36cl (David Fleetham), 22tr (David Hall), 17b (Howard Hall), 44cl (Richard Herrmann), 18tr (Rudie Kuiter), 8c, 9cr, 19tr, 32bc, 35tr, 39cr, 41br, 60tr (Doug Perrine), 56tr (Todd Pusser), 16bcr (Bruce Rasner), 55c (David Shen), 39tl (Marty Snyderman), 12bl (Walt Stearns), 40tr (Mark Strickland), 32cl, 38tr (James D. Watt), 13c (David Wrobel). **Michelle Jeffries/Naval Ocean Systems** 31cr. **Leighton Taylor** 16bl. **Marine Mammal Images** 21c (Tershy and Strong). **James Marks** 27cr, 40bl. **Monterey Bay Aquarium** 55bc. **Connie Lyn Morgan** 42bl. **Skip Naftel/ Ocean Surveys** 20bc. **National Geographic Society Image Collection** 49tl (Nick Caloyianis). **Ocean Earth Images** 30tc (David Hempenstall). **Pacific Stock** 15br (Darodents). **The Photo Library, Sydney** 52tr (Tony Stone Images/Aldo Brando). **Photo Resource, Hawaii** 61br (Christina Beauchamp). **Dr Andreas Rechnitzer** 56bl. **Jeff Rotman** 11tr, 30tr. **Science Photo Library** 28cl (Eye of Science), 58cl (Simon Fraser). **Tom Stack and Associates** 11br (Tom and Therisa Stack), 25bc (Patrice Ceisel). **Still Pictures** 57tc (Jeff Rotman). **The Sydney Aquarium, Darling Harbour** 53br. **Twilight Zone Photographics** 45cr (Mark Spencer). **Senzu Uchida** 38bl. **Waterhouse** 14tr (Stephen Frink), 19cr (Chris Newbert), 60cl (Marty Snyderman). **R. Woodward** 45br. **www.norbertwu.com** 12tr (1999/James Watt/Mo Yung Productions), 29tr (1999/Norbert Wu).

**ILLUSTRATION CREDITS Martin Camm** 7tr, 16/17tc, 16tl, 16tc, 17tr, 17cr, 17bl, 40/41b, 40cl, 40cr, 40t, 41c, 62tr, 63tl, 63br. **Marjorie Crosby-Fairall** 4cr, 6tr, 10/11c, 10bl, 11b, 17br, 26br, 27tc, 27bc, 27br, 34/35c, 34/35b, 34tl, 34tr, 44/45c, 44b, 44t, 45b, 63bc. **Marc Dando/Wildlife Art Ltd** 4tr, 18/19c, 18t, 18bl, 19bl, 19br, 22/23c, 22b, 22t, 23b, 38/39c, 38t, 39c, 39cr. **Ray Grinaway** 6cr, 7cr, 12/13c, 12t, 12b, 13bl, 13tr, 21tr, 47cl, 47br, 58/59c, 58t, 59tr, 60/61c, 60b, 60t, 61b, 63tc. **Gino Hasler** 26tr, 26cr, 26ecr, 28/29c, 28t, 28bl, 29b, 30/31c, 30cr, 30b, 31bl, 31br, 31cl, 32/33c, 32t, 33br, 33bl. **Ian Jackson/Wildlife Art Ltd.** 4bc, 14/15c, 14t, 15cr, 27tr, 36/37c, 36t, 37r, 46tr, 47tr, 48/49c, 48l, 48t, 49r, 56/57c, 56t, 56b, 57r, 63bl. **Roger Swainston** 4etr, 6etr, 8/9c, 8t, 8b, 9bl, 9br, 20/21c, 20tl, 21r, 27bl, 42bl, 42t, 42br, 43c, 43r, 46br, 47tl, 50/51c, 50/51b, 50t, 52/53c, 52/53b, 52t, 54/55c, 54bl, 54t, 54br, 55r, 62tc, 62bl, 62br, 63tr. **Chris Turnbull/Wildlife Art Ltd** 6br, 7br, 24/25c, 24bc, 24cl, 24bl, 24t, 25tr, 25tc, 25br, 25cr, 62tl.

**COVER CREDITS** Auscape International FCc (Ben & Lynn Cropp). **Marjorie Crosby-Fairall** BCtl, BCbl, Fft, FCcl, FCtr, FCbl, FCbc, FCebr. **Marc Dando/Wildlife Art Ltd** Ffcr, Ffcl. **Ray Grinaway** BCbc, FCtc, FCebcl, FCcl. **Ian Jackson/Wildlife Art Ltd** Bft, Bfb, BCc, FCebr. **Roger Swainston** Bfc, BCetr, BCcr, FCtl, Ffc, Ffb, FCcr. **Chris Turnbull/Wildlife Art Ltd** BCcl, BCtr, BCbr, FCc, FCebl.